This gem of a book is what I want to give to absolutely every family I know. Intentional, formational, biblical, with profound generational—and eternal—ramifications, Earley hands us transformational hope for every single family with these practical and gospel-saturated pages. I couldn't put it down.

—Ann Voskamp, mother of seven, author of the *New York Times* bestsellers *One Thousand Gifts* and *The Broken Way*

If you've never considered how a liturgy could include children bouncing on their beds or cooling down after a meltdown or passing the pepper around the dinner table (and I never had), this book could help you change the habits of your home. It never nags, scolds, guilts, or mandates. Instead, Justin Earley suggests ways that people like you and me—people with piled-up dishes and maddening soccer schedules and too little confidence that we know what we're doing—can build habits to equip our families for the lifelong pilgrimage toward Home.

—Russell Moore, *Christianity Today*

Parents need this book! Rhythms are paramount in our families, and Justin offers insights on how practicing them at home displays Jesus to our children in ways words alone cannot.

—Rebekah Lyons, bestselling author, *Rhythms of Renewal* and *You Are Free*

The family is God's primary discipleship plan. It is in our households that we are taught what is most important and least important and we begin to understand how we fit in this big and scary world. In *Habits of the Household*, Justin Whitmel Earley gives us a template for household habits that root our families in the deepest realities of the gospel of Jesus Christ and form all of us more into his image. There is no formation without repetition, so I pray this book encourages your heart and emboldens your desire to allow the Spirit to flow into and through these ten everyday occurrences with greater purpose and intentionality.

—Matt Chandler, lead pastor, The Vill-- -

If you are a parent, or about to be one, or a friend of one, or a parent of one, this is gold. Sheer, honest, hilarious, helpful family-shaping gold. There is nothing easy about this most vulnerable of human vocations, and the habits in this book will not make it easy. But they will make it so much better.

—ANDY CROUCH, author, *The Tech-Wise Family*

I got no farther than the introduction and was already implementing these practices with my kids! Such a thoughtful, practical, humble, yet hilarious look at pulling out the sacred in the everyday chaos of parenting. These practices will become staples in our home.

—JOSHUA STRAUB, PhD, *Famous at Home*

Through the last nineteen years of parenting, I've viewed parenting books with a mix of fear and loathing. It seems like "experts" were quick to tell me what I was doing wrong and to offer quick-fix solutions that felt removed from my actual messy, relentless, inconsistent experience as a parent. That's why reading Justin's *Habits of the Household* was such a refreshing, inspiring experience. Justin has managed to boil down the complex world of parenting into a series of relevant, grace-filled, realistic habits that will change the formation of your family. I found myself creating a mental list of every young parent I couldn't wait to gift this book. A must-read for every parent longing to bring more meaning to their daily life.

—NICOLE UNICE, pastor, leadership consultant, and author of *The Miracle Moment: How Tough Conversations Can Actually Transform Your Most Important Relationships*

What a timely and helpful resource! I only wish I had read this when my children were still at home. In *Habits of the Household*, Justin helps us consider our normal and ordinary lives, and how powerfully formative simple practices can be. This is not a how-to book but rather a grace-filled approach to life at home that helps us see habituation as freeing and fruitful. I can't wait to buy a box and give copies to parents.

—KEITH NIX, Veritas School, Richmond, VA; national leader in classical Christian education renewal movement

I met Justin Earley fifteen years ago; we were fresh out of college serving together as missionaries overseas. Even then, I could tell he had wisdom beyond his years. And ever since, I have been encouraged to watch him develop his voice for the benefit of Christ's people. It's no secret that home life can be chaotic—many of us are in its throes now, settling for survival mode as we simply try to make it through the day. We want to form our kids with Christian virtue, but sometimes the fight can feel futile. *Habits of the Household* will help you implement rhythms that will bring order to the mess and grace in the stress.

—MATT SMETHURST, planting pastor, River City Baptist Church, Richmond, VA; managing editor, The Gospel Coalition; author, *Deacons* and *Before You Open Your Bible*

HABITS OF THE HOUSEHOLD

JUSTIN WHITMEL EARLEY

HABITS OF THE HOUSEHOLD

PRACTICING THE STORY OF GOD

IN EVERYDAY FAMILY RHYTHMS

ZONDERVAN
BOOKS

ZONDERVAN BOOKS

Habits of the Household
Copyright © 2021 by Avodah, LLC

Published in Grand Rapids, Michigan, by Zondervan. Zondervan is a registered trademark of The Zondervan Corporation, L.L.C., a wholly owned subsidary of HarperCollins Christian Publishing, Inc.

Requests for information should be addressed to customercare@harpercollins.com.

Zondervan titles may be purchased in bulk for educational, business, fundraising, or sales promotional use. For information, please email SpecialMarkets@Zondervan.com.

ISBN 978-0-310-36296-8 (audio)

Library of Congress Cataloging-in-Publication Data

Names: Earley, Justin Whitmel, 1984- author.
Title: Habits of the household : practicing the story of God in everyday family rhythms / Justin Whitmel Earley.
Description: Grand Rapids : Zondervan, 2021. | Includes bibliographical references. | Summary: "Habits of the Household by award-winning author Justin Whitmel Earley equips you with simple habits for mealtimes, bedtimes, and other daily routines to shape your home in the rhythms of God's love"— Provided by publisher.
Identifiers: LCCN 2021029651 | ISBN 9780310362937 (trade paperback) | ISBN 9780310362944 (ebook)
Subjects: LCSH: Households—Religious aspects Christianity. | Families—Religious life. | Parenting—Religious aspects Christianity.
Classification: LCC BV4526.3 .E25 2021 | DDC 248.4—dc23
LC record available at https://lccn.loc.gov/2021029651

Published in association with Don Gates of the literary agency The Gates Group, www .the-gates-group.com.

Cover design: Micah Kandros
Cover illustrations: Shutterstock
Author photo: James Lee
Interior design: Denise Froehlich

Printed in the United States of America

24 25 26 27 28 LBC 23 22 21 20 19

To Whit, Asher, Coulter, and Shep

———

"Because it is easier to raise strong children
than to repair broken men and women"

CONTENTS

FOREWORD

We all face a constant challenge to be present in the moment. At any given time, it's easy for our thoughts to be all over the place—thinking about a pending task, mulling over an email we received, or even daydreaming about being somewhere other than where we are. Truly being present in the moment is important, but often elusive—even in our parenting. We often complete the tasks of family life on autopilot while our minds wander.

Have you ever gotten to the end of a busy day and realized that you were essentially dragged through it by the demands you live under? What about the challenge of organizing your family's day around God's Word? Or navigating technology with your kids? The electronic distractions that we grew up with pale in comparison with the leviathan of social media!

Whether it's our divided attention, the chaotic pace of any given day, or the challenges of technology, the longer we live in unhealthy patterns, the more normal they can seem. But in our more sober reflective moments, we realize that something needs to change. The question is what? And how?

With nineteen years of parenting six boys under our belts, Ruth and I have learned many lessons about organizing home life. In all we do, we work to keep Christ and the gospel at the center of our focus. We've found that discipling our boys doesn't happen at a specific time each day; rather it has become the framework we use throughout the entire day. Discipling happens in the context of the habits we form and the rhythms we keep.

So just like Moses commanded the Israelites in Deuteronomy 6, we try to talk about the Word of God all day long, encouraging one another to walk by it. If you share a meal with us, you'll likely hear our boys pray, "May all we say and do bring honor and glory to you." Though my heart swells when I hear them pray those words, I also know it won't be long before someone loses patience and speaks an unkind word—such is the way of every day in the Simons household.

In the midst of everyday challenges—big and small—Ruth and I are so thankful for the wisdom that Justin shares in this book. He reminds us that habits and rhythms have power, and helps tackle the questions surrounding intentional living and parenting. If you feel like life is moving at a frenetic pace and you're struggling to keep your own heart centered, let alone your family's, this book is strong medicine. In straightforward and candid fashion, Justin breaks down the activities of a day, giving wise instruction for how to reclaim the time we're losing for maximum gospel impact in our homes.

Regardless of where you are when you start this book, be encouraged that it *is* possible to establish new rhythms, even today—because God isn't through with us yet.

—RUTH CHOU SIMONS AND TROY SIMONS,
bestselling authors of *Foundations: Twelve
Biblical Truths to Shape a Family*

INTRODUCTION

REIMAGINING HOUSEHOLD
HABITS AS GOSPEL LITURGIES

It was 8:00 p.m. on a Wednesday evening, and bedtime with our boys was not going well. Nothing was particularly wrong, but nothing was particularly right, either.

It was more of what most nights were: two had fled the bath and begun a spontaneous wrestling match, Greco-Roman style (that is, naked), on the floor of their bedroom. The youngest had gotten involved by turning his board books into projectiles, apparently trying to break the match up by knocking one of the older two out.

I had recently left my job at an international law firm and started my own business-law practice. Lauren was pregnant with our fourth boy, because clearly our house needed more Greco-Roman wrestlers. Life was then, as it still is now, fairly high paced.

On the way to the bathroom, I was debating whether I should get back to one of my clients, who was in the middle of an investment round, or first clean the kitchen. I was also wracking my brain trying to remember whose toothbrush was the Superman one and whose was the T. rex one, because if I got this wrong, there was going to be more gnashing of teeth than brushing.

This was all interrupted when I almost slipped on some bathwater they had trailed onto the creaking floorboards of our hundred-year-old house in Richmond, Virginia. I barely avoided a wipeout by catching myself on a doorknob that almost shook loose, and that's when the switch flips. I don't "run out" of patience nearly so much as I decide that I'm out of patience.

The next ten minutes are a blur. I'm barking orders and moving bodies from one place to another. But it doesn't actually speed anything up; it just makes us all tense. In such moments, I begin to feel like an impotent general shouting commands that, despite their volume, seem to have little effect on anything. Things like, "I don't care, you are using this toothbrush!" And, "I pulled the book out of your hands because you weren't listening to me." Or, "No more drinks of water! We're done with water."

Finally, I reach the moment I've been waiting for. I turn the lights out and shut the door. But as I stood in the upstairs hallway, still damp with bathwater, I didn't feel the usual relief of bedtime being over. I felt conflicted and embarrassed.

I was thinking about how this was a normal night, which means their last image of me most days is of this wild taskmaster raging about how if they don't get pj's on this instant there will be dramatic physical consequences. I wondered if they sensed the irony when, before turning out the lights, I gave them a short bedtime prayer and told them that God loves them and I do too. I wondered what they think love means.

I'm not sure why this night was the occasion for my epiphany, because it certainly wasn't an unusual evening. In fact, it was typical, which is exactly what led to my epiphany: "This is our normal," I murmured to myself. And that wasn't a good thing.

The Significance of What's Normal

One of the most significant things about any household is what is considered to be normal. Moments aggregate, and they become memories and tradition. Our routines become who we are, become the story and culture of our families.

Standing in the hallway that night, I wasn't disappointed with my evening nearly so much as I was disappointed with my ordinary. One night is one thing. A norm is another.

Some weeks later, I was discussing our nightly chaos with one of my pastors, Derek, and he suggested I try a bedtime liturgy. "What's that?" I said. He shared with me one he does with his boys, and I was intrigued.

The idea of a bedtime liturgy sounded strange at first, but the more I thought about it the more it made sense. A liturgy, in the formal sense, is a pattern of worship we repeat over and over, hoping that the pattern draws us into worship and forms us in the image of the one we worship. This wasn't totally new to me. In fact, I had been using time outside of my law practice to write about how habits of work and technology are really patterns of worship that deeply form us.[1] I had thought a lot about the spiritual significance of daily habits functioning as liturgies; but honestly, I just hadn't really applied this insight to parenting and children.

But when Derek mentioned a bedtime liturgy, the realization clicked—my parenting was already filled with liturgies, just not ones that I had chosen carefully. These small patterns I had with Lauren and the boys—our waking, our meals, our car rides, our bedtimes—were all moments of worship too, guided by habits that could accurately be seen as liturgies. Liturgies of what? Now that I thought about it, probably liturgies of efficiency, impatience, rush, or frustration. These rhythms were certainly not ones I would choose, but they were the ones we had, and that needed to change.

---

1. Justin Whitmel Earley, *The Common Rule: Habits of Purpose for an Age of Distraction* (Downers Grove, IL: InterVarsity, 2019).

It was in this mix of both frustration and inspiration that I wrote my first nighttime blessing for the boys. I hoped it could be a little liturgy for sending them off to sleep and perhaps interrupt the liturgy of impatience I was defaulting to.

Here's what I wrote:

A BEDTIME BLESSING OF GOSPEL LOVE

Said perhaps with a hand on your child's face or head.

Parent: Do you see my eyes?
Child: Yes.
Parent: Can you see that I see your eyes?
Child: Yes.
Parent: Do you know that I love you?
Child: Yes.
Parent: Do you know that I love you no matter what bad things you do?
Child: Yes.
Parent: Do you know that I love you no matter what good things you do?
Child: Yes.
Parent: Who else loves you like that?
Child: God does.
Parent: Even more than me?
Child: Yes.
Parent: Rest in that love.

You can imagine how well this went the first time.

It didn't. Not at all.

They were confused. They were suddenly very interested in

what it meant that I could see their eyes. They took it as an invitation to poke my eyes. Suddenly eye contact was hilarious, and so on. Fortunately, by this time in my parenting career I was used to the humor, nonsense, and skirmishes that inevitably punctuate attempts at serious and spiritual moments with children. So I kept on.

Often, I forgot what I had planned to say. Sometimes I brought notes. And even after a couple of nights of practice, there was still general confusion about what was happening. But I knew from my research and writing on habits that this is exactly what it looks like every time you start a new routine. Nothing is normal until it is. At the risk of stating the obvious, the significance of a family pattern is that it's not just a moment. It is not something you do once and say, "Well, that went swimmingly!" or, "That was rough." It's a routine you practice, whether consciously or unconsciously.

After a few days of practice, a remarkable moment happened. In the midst of an equally messy evening, one of the boys, finally lying in bed, asked, "Can we have our blessing now?"

It was the point where something we've done became something we do. A habit of the household was born.

That night, I looked into their eyes, and they looked into mine, and we exchanged a brief word about God's remarkable love for us—the love he offers us in spite of our bad parenting habits and our good ones, in spite of our best days and our worst days, in spite of our proudest moments and in spite of our darkest secrets, his love never changes. For just a moment, and in kid language, we talked about this remarkable and unconditional love of God for us.

To be clear, except for this moment, this night was exactly like all the other ones. It was still chaos and there was still bathwater on the floor, but it was also punctuated by a bright spot of meaning. And that seemed to make all the difference.

A couple of years later, it still does.

We now have four boys, and a nighttime blessing is a keystone habit of our evening routine. That said, board books are still weapons, naked wrestling matches are still more common than I'd prefer, toothbrushes are still the most sacred of household property rights, and I still spend a significant amount of time evaluating my life in hallways. But the thing that is different is—well, me. The circumstances are mostly the same, but my reaction to them has dramatically changed. And that is the power of a good parenting habit: by changing our knee-jerk reactions to ordinary situations, we uncover different ways of letting God's grace guide our hearts—and our children's hearts—into new patterns of life together.

This may be counterintuitive at first. It was for me. We don't often think about habits and the heart being so interconnected. But they are. To steward the habits of your family is to steward the hearts of your family.

And that's what this book is about.

The Heart Follows the Habit

"You're going to love school today," I tell Whit as I zip up his coat. "You have PE, which means you get to go outside," I go on as I tie his shoes. "And if you see your brother Ash in the hallway, make sure you give him a fist bump," I remind him as I buckle his seat belt, "because brothers stick together, okay?"

This is a remarkable moment, and totally normal. You do it too. We do complicated, difficult tasks on autopilot. We flip pancakes and change diapers while also doing much more important things like chatting with a spouse or mulling over a work problem. We can do this because of the amazing phenomenon of habit.

Habits are fascinating little things. They are the things we do over and over, semiconsciously to unconsciously. By definition, they are, of course, little. But the aggregate impact of habits is as big as each habit is small. Habits not only occupy most of our time, they form most of our minds. There is a neurological reason for this.

Modern neuroscience has shown us that habits occur in the deepest parts of our brains, the basal ganglia, which are the parts that churn on autopilot while the higher order thinking does its complex acrobatics.

This is wonderful because it frees up our higher order thinking for more important things. This is why I can tie shoes and buckle seat belts while also teaching an important lesson to Whit about how brothers are to show affection in public.

On the other hand, you can see the absence of habit's magic when you watch a toddler try to tie their own shoe—the task consumes every bit of mental energy they have. You could not break through if you were a bear on a unicycle.

This capacity of our brains to work in lower order habit while higher order thinking cruises along uninterrupted is one of God's wonderful neurological gifts to us.[2] When done right, we can accumulate all kinds of wonderful processes in our lower order thinking, and they become completely natural to us: the drive home, a hug on the way out the door, a nighttime blessing, a dinner table prayer, catching a football, cracking an egg,

---

2. I will refer to the difference between lower and higher order thinking throughout the book. Sometimes I will also refer to the upstairs brain and the downstairs brain. In general, the lower part of the brain is the part that handles basic, ongoing, and survival-oriented tasks like fight or flight, and rest and digest. Meanwhile, the upper brain helps us do the more sophisticated work of being human like using logic, processing new information, and solving complicated problems. I will summarize the key takeaways, but if you want more on how these parts of our brains affect our life of habit, see Charles Duhigg, *The Power of Habit: Why We Do What We Do in Life and Business* (New York: Random House, 2012).

or rubbing your spouse's neck. Whether rote or romantic, habits allow us to carry on in a world that's plenty complicated enough without needing to second-guess ourselves constantly.

But the neurological downside of habits is as powerful as the upside. The same feature that allows us to perform a good habit without thinking about it makes it hard to change a bad habit even when we are thinking about it. Picture a wagon wheel in a rut. It takes no effort at all to stay in the rut. But it takes incredible effort to pull the wheel out of it.

Good or bad, a rut is a rut, and our brains love ruts.

Your basal ganglia are so good at staying in the rut that you cannot just tell them to get out. Your lower brain has spent its whole life ignoring that higher order thinking. It's supposed to, after all. Its job is to keep you in the rut regardless.

In other words: *You can't think yourself out of a pattern you didn't think yourself into.* You practiced yourself into it, so you have to practice your way out.

Take my nighttime routine. I knew in my higher order brain that I didn't want to spend another evening barking orders at my children. But when I slipped on the water in the hallway, the basal ganglia (which house the fight or flight response) were triggered, and I flipped into the habit of fighting my way through the evening. The norm unfolded not just without much thought but even in spite of my thought.

This is why habits are so neurologically formative: like a rut, they take us somewhere. They have a destination even when our minds are opposed to it.

But habits are not just neurologically formative. Habits are also spiritually formative.

Because when our heads go one way but our habits go another, guess which way the heart follows?

The heart always follows the habit.

Seeing Ordinary Habits as Liturgies of Worship

Why? Because habits are kinds of liturgies. They are little routines of worship, and worship changes what we love. Habits of the household are not just actions that form our families' routines, they are liturgies that form our families' hearts. This is why we should choose them so carefully.

Think of it like this: when it comes to spiritual formation, our households are not simply products of what we teach and say. They are much more products of what we practice and do. And usually there is a significant gap between the two.

If our hearts always followed our heads, we would not need to practice the things we learn. We'd just learn about it and the rest would follow. But that's not how humans work, which is why the biblical understanding of sanctification is not just about education and learning but about formation and practice as well.[3] We are tasked not only with learning the right thing, which takes concentration and thinking,[4] but also with practicing the right things, which takes formation and repetition.[5]

Consider habits of the household as an effort to unite education and formation. Think about them as ways to align our heads and our hearts so we don't just know the right thing to do, *we also love doing the right thing.*

The neurology and spirituality of habits can seem complicated (especially if you haven't thought about any of this before), but few matters are more practical than the spirituality of habit.

---

3. Phil. 4:9: "Whatever you have learned or received or heard from me, or seen in me—put it into practice. And the God of peace will be with you."
4. Prov. 4:6–7, for example, or the emphasis on knowledge and understanding in Col. 1:9–10.
5. Prov. 22:6, for example, or the complementary emphasis on growing in good works in Col. 1:9–10.

Here are some examples of how I've seen the interplay between my head, my heart, and my habits in my parenting life:

WAYS NEW HABITS LEAD THE HEART	
My Head Thinks ... I want to be a patient person with my kids.	
My Old Habit Leads My Heart... But my default habit is to reprimand them for every spill, which leads to an impatient mood of constantly snapping at them.	**Until a New Habit Leads My Heart...** Until I cultivated the habit of always saying (often through gritted teeth), "That's okay. Why don't you help me clean it up?" Saying this paves the way to a shared cleanup process instead of another reprimand. I *feel* more patient because I *practice* talking patiently.
My Head Thinks ... I want to give my kids my full attention.	
My Old Habit Leads My Heart... But the morning news notifications on my phone always get me mad and worried. I'm usually absent and distracted through the morning as we get the kids out the door.	**Until a New Habit Leads My Heart...** Until I cultivated the habit of turning off all notifications and not using my phone before drop-off. We are formed in the image of what we habitually gaze at. The habits of our hearts follow the habits of our phones.
My Head Thinks ... I want to use moments of discipline to teach my kids, not just be angry at them.	
My Old Habit Leads My Heart... But my constant reaction is just to get mad and yell when they act out in the same ways over and over.	**Until a New Habit Leads My Heart...** Until I practiced the habit of pausing and praying before I discipline. I didn't realize that I am the one who needs a timeout. The prayerful pause doesn't make what they did right, but it helps my heart remember I'm a broken and needy child of God, just like they are. A carefully chosen habit for my kids changes my heart for my kids.

My Head Thinks ... I want to pray for my kids.	
My Old Habit Leads My Heart...	**Until a New Habit Leads My Heart...**
But it just never happens. I worry a lot for them, but I never actually pray.	Until I practiced the habit of praying at their door each night before I get into bed. Sure, it is only a minute or so, but I realize that while my heart isn't good at spontaneously praying for them, it was very good at getting into a nightly routine of praying for them.

I will unpack all of these examples more in the chapters to come, but notice that just like me, most parents *want* to be patient, attentive, and loving parents who pray for their kids and show them gentleness. But until our hopes make their way from our heads to our habits, nothing changes. The idea of the parents we want to be remains stuck in our minds, and our kids suffer for that.

But it doesn't have to be that way. It is possible to practice habits of the household that lead our hearts, and our children's hearts, in new directions.

That said, let me also be careful and clear. This book will not claim that there are some easy life hacks that can kickstart your best parenting life in a couple of days. Nothing important is easy. So I will not claim that rethinking the habits of our households is easy in any sense. But what I will claim is that these habits profoundly matter to our families' spiritual formation, and changing them is possible.

It may be the most important thing you do as a parent.

Habits of the Household as a "Rule of Life"

The idea that we should be attentive to our communal habits is not new. Not at all. There is an ancient monastic term for this idea. It's called a "rule of life." A rule of life is a pattern of shared habits intended to shape a community in the love of God.

The concept of a rule of life gains some of its roots from the story of Daniel and the way he and his fellow servants insisted that while they would serve in Babylon's courts, they would follow a different pattern of living. Their commitment to specific habits of eating, drinking, and praying (their rule of life) is what allowed them to be "in the world, but not of it."[6]

We see a similar idea in the early Christian church described in Acts 2. Early believers' conversions led them to adopt habits radically different from the world around them.[7] The distinctiveness of their habits set them apart, called them to the commitments of their faith, and attracted many others to join them.

The idea that our faith should lead us to commit to communal habits was formalized in the monasteries of famous church fathers like St. Augustine and St. Benedict, each of whom wrote a rule of life for their monasteries. If you read these wonderful documents, and you should, you will find them equal parts inspiring and eccentric. Some of the habits are nitpicky (like how much wine should be allocated to a monk),[8] some of them are awe-inspiring commitments to community and friendship (like Augustine's "whenever you go out, walk together, and when you reach your destination, stay together"),[9] and many others are exactly what you would expect—rhythms of prayer, Scripture reading, and eating together.

But what you can't miss if you read these rules is the thing that motivated them: *love*. Daniel, the early church, and the monastics all were simply living out Jesus' summary of the law—the

---

6. The phrase often used to summarize John 17:14–19.
7. Acts 2:42–47.
8. *Rule of St. Benedict*, chapter 40.
9. *Rule of St. Augustine*, chapter IV, sentence 2.

essence of Christian life is loving God and loving neighbor. Out of centuries of this tradition of communities choosing their communal habits carefully, a new phrase began to grow: "the school of love." All kinds of spiritual communities have used this phrase since, and with good reason.

The most Christian way to think about our households is that they are little "schools of love," places where we have one vocation, one calling: to form all who live here into lovers of God and neighbor.

This is not a works-based legalistic endeavor, it's a grace-based beautiful one.

When brothers and sisters who came before us set out to form communal habits, they weren't trying to prove or earn anything. They were trying to create a framework of habit on which the love of God and neighbor could grow. In fact, the Latin root for the word *rule* didn't mean a law you had to obey. It connoted a bar or a trellis—a framework that allows life to flourish.

These communities realized that if they didn't shape their trellis of habit, the world would shape one for them. They were saying, "If we don't have radical communal habits to form us, we will end up conforming to the communal patterns of the world around us."

They saw with clear eyes that their world was malforming people into typical Babylonians and Romans. Lives that were blind to seeing God for who he is. Lives that were ordered around the love of self, the love of power, the love of riches, and the love of sex. Lives that look, from our perspective, suspiciously American.

The phrase *rule of life* might be new to you, but the concept is not. We all have a set of communal habits we are defaulting to. But most of our families are defaulting to the American set of habits, the American rule of life.

By not choosing our habits carefully, we are falling back on rhythms that are forming us in all of the usual patterns of unceasing screentime, unending busyness, unrivaled consumerism, unrelenting loneliness, unmitigated addictions, and unparalleled distraction.

"Systems are perfectly designed to get the results they are getting," so say the business gurus.[10] Our contemporary system of cultural habits is the same. The cultural default is perfectly designed to produce the kinds of families it is producing. We are familiar with them. So why would we, as Christians called to be ambassadors of Christ, default to this American rule of life?

In suggesting that we reconsider our habits of the household, I am suggesting that we reclaim the idea of creating a rule of life in our families so we can produce something other than the typical anxiety-ridden, depression-prone, lonely, confused, and screen-addicted teenager. So we can form children in God's love. So we can train them in meaningful relationships. So we can teach them the peace that comes with knowing the unconditional love of Jesus. So we can create homes that are missional lights in a dark world.

We need a household rule of life if we are to become families that love the world like God loves us. This is an urgent matter for our families, and it's also an urgent matter of neighbor love. We cannot be the lovers of God and neighbor we are called to be without examining the habits of the household.

Being Parented by God

I'm in the hallway again, but this time it's before I go to bed, and I'm praying at their door. This is another little habit that was born

---

10. Quote often attributed to W. Edwards Deming.

half from intention and half from desperation. I often visit their door in the evening before sleeping and say something like this: "God, please parent me so I can parent them."

It is years later now, and the more I've thought about habits and formation in the family, the more I've realized how connected we are. My habits are forming me into a certain kind of parent. My parenting is forming them into certain kinds of children. We are all, together, forming each other into a certain kind of family.

There is no escaping habits and formation in the family. We become our habits, and our kids become us. The family, for better or worse, is a formation machine.

The stakes are high, and if all we looked at is what we're doing as a family, this talk about habits would be an incredible burden.

But not if we look up. When we look up, we see that we have a heavenly father, a divine parent who is parenting us. He is forming us into perfectly loved children of the King. We do not have to invent anything, carry anything, or bear the final burden of parenting. We just get to follow someone.

The Christian posture toward habits of the household is not about carrying our families on our backs and hiking up the steep mountain of life. It is much more childlike than that. It is simply about taking hold of the outstretched hand of our heavenly Father and following him, one baby step at a time.

Our best parenting comes when we think less about being parents of children and more about being children of God.

So don't worry. Rethinking the habits of your household isn't a heavy burden. What's heavy is continuing to do nothing. What's burdensome is continuing to follow default cultural habits. But taking the hand of God and being willing to follow him wherever he leads—that's light. It's the posture of a child.

Someone who is stronger than you and who loves you is in charge. And that's good news for parents *and* children.

HOW TO READ THIS BOOK

———

M y greatest hope is not that you sit down in a quiet place and read this book alone. You might do that with a good novel, but this book is quite a bit different. It's not so much full of things to read as it is full of things to try.

So I hope, rather, that you read snatches of it between toddler fits and soccer trips. I hope that you nod off during a chapter because the baby was up last night, and get distracted at a good part because your twelve-year-old drops a surprise question about sex. I hope that you read a page aloud for your spouse, then put it down and talk about it. I hope that you stop between chapters and try out a habit, and then make notes when it doesn't work quite like you thought it would. I hope that you skip around because you feel good about where family mealtimes are but feel lost at sea when it comes to moments of discipline. I hope that you read it in groups of parents who are comfortable enough to admit that none of us really knows what we're doing, so we can talk honestly about it, without judgment. I hope that you spill coffee on it or milk on it or tea on it or wine on it. I hope you argue with your spouse (just a little bit) over whether these habits matter and why. I hope it gets left dog-eared on your kitchen counter and stuffed in your diaper bag.

That would be the highest honor, because that means that this book is in the hands of the right person. A parent in a messy house. A parent in the trenches. A parent like me.

I write this book to parents in the thick of it because I am a parent in the thick of it myself.

I Write from a Messy House

This morning I woke to crumbs on the kitchen floor and used up the last of the milk. Last night one of the boys (who will remain unnamed) pulled his pants down during family devotions (or almost did—I caught him just in time). Right now laundry is on the kitchen table, the yard needs some serious work, and I am postponing a work call to type this paragraph. We are overwhelmed, and that's not unusual for us.

Yesterday, Lauren texted me asking for extra prayer because the boys were "so hard." I texted back, "Will pray. I get it—me too," and I wasn't just feigning sympathy. I actually did stop and pray because I think I actually do get it.

Parenting is really hard, mostly messy, and none of us shines at it.

At best, I am a tired, confused, impatient, guilt-ridden, and regret-prone father whose only hope is that Jesus actually did live, die, and rise again. My only hope is that grace means that that divine reality will somehow break into my reality. Because my reality is that I don't feel like I'm good at my job as a parent.

The good news is that the more I talk to parents, the more I realize that we all feel the same way! I've learned Mandarin Chinese, graduated with honors from a top law school, passed the bar exam, practiced mergers and acquisitions at international law firms, worked my way out of the anxiety crashes that those firms tend to cause, written books and started my own business—and I still think that parenting is hands down the hardest thing I've ever done.

So I admittedly (and unashamedly) write from the trenches.

And we might as well level on that. During the time of my writing this book, my four boys ranged in age from one to nine, and it has not been easy.

If you want to picture a parent who has it all together and can tell you how to do it right, let me as politely as possible show you to the door. I am not that person.

But you might as well know that no one else is either.

This means, mercifully, that we can all stop the guilt and the judging. Our conversation in this book, I hope, is like the place the church is meant to be: a place for recovering sinners to rejoice that we are all fouled up but God loves us anyway. So it is that I write about habits of the household from a messy household.

Some of these sentences were written downstairs before the kids woke. Others were scribbled on a pad when I should have been clearing the table. Some were typed at the office while I snoozed a couple of client emails, and some were hastily tapped out on my phone in the middle of a backyard fire conversation among friends sharing our mutual parenting struggles. But all of them come from the fray, and all of them are much more scuffed up by failure than they are polished up by success.

I find I am drawn to write about things I struggle with, and habits of the household are no different. I'm qualified to write about this stuff not because I'm so good at it, I'm qualified to write about this stuff because I need it so badly.

How This Book Is Structured

One of the central themes of this book is that we become our habits, and our kids become us. Which means who our children are becoming is tightly connected to who we are becoming—personally and communally. For that reason, when we think about Christian formation in a household, we are thinking in at least three directions: forming parents, forming children, and forming a family. As you can see in figure 1, the chapters will unfold in habits that might occur throughout a day, but each habit will have an emphasis on forming parents, children, or families.

Figure 1

| FORMING PARENTS | FORMING FAMILIES | FORMING CHILDREN |

Forming Parents

Parenting your children is not just about what you are doing in their lives. It is first about the work God is doing in your life. This means the starting point of parenting habits is thinking about how our household habits are forming us as parents. We can't make disciples without being disciples. We can't teach the grace of God outside of experiencing the grace of God.

So some of these chapters—habits of waking or habits of marriage, for example—will be directed at you. These habits remind me that I can't be a good father if I'm not a good husband. I can't be a committed father if I'm not a committed disciple. There is a certain primacy to these habits. I've placed them at the beginning and middle of the book to serve as weights to balance the content. We need spiritual rhythms to become the kind of people God calls us to be before we can think about the kind of parents God calls us to be.

Forming Children

I feel a certain awe when I am surrounded by children. Whether this is playing in the back yard with the neighborhood kids or sitting at the dinner table with my sons, I sometimes suddenly remember that we parents get the fearsome and awesome opportunity to shape human beings. Sometimes this makes me cry, because I want so badly to protect them all and I know I can't. Sometimes it makes me proud, because I feel I have the most important job in the world. Other times I don't even know where to start, because it is such an overwhelming responsibility. I think all of these responses have a place. Forming children is wonderful, scary, and altogether too much, which is why we need help.

After the habits of forming parents, half of the remaining habits are about forming children. These chapters focus on the areas where we get to pick the routines that shape our children: bedtimes, moments of discipline, screentime, and family devotions. There is a real practicality and primacy to these habits, because so much of our day-to-day is concerned with them. For that reason, you'll notice that these chapters contain a bit more depth and length.

Forming Families

Finally, at the intersection of forming parents and forming children is family culture. This is the idea that when we come together, something unique happens—a household is born. These chapters will be about habits that focus on communal formation—things like mealtimes, conversations, and rhythms of work and play.

You will notice an outward nature to these habits. These are the places where the household begins to move out into the world, or in some cases, where the household invites the world in. For example, one way to think about family culture is to think about what habits and norms our friends and neighbors are invited into when they come over. Another way to think about family culture is what we send out into the world when we befriend others and do our work in the world. In both senses, these habits of forming families look beyond the doorstep of the household and peer out into the world of loving neighbors and being a light to the world.

The Spirituality of Domestic Life

In real life, forming parents, forming children, and forming families all blend during a typical day. For that reason, the order of these chapters will unfold not categorically but rather as a day might. We will begin with morning and end with bedtime. In between we'll look at work and play and meals and discipline. Feel free to skip to a chapter that interests you, because each of them stands alone. However, you will find that if you take them in order, the themes build on each other.

In following the ordinary pace of a day, I hope to draw your attention over and over to one of the other central themes of this book: *that the greatest spiritual work happens in the normal moments of domestic life.*

On the one hand, I hope you find this encouraging. Realizing that the normal moments of life are also the most spiritual moments of life helps give a validity and dignity to the otherwise mundane and repetitive nature of housework and parenting. I know we parents constantly wonder whether all of this matters, and I will try to assure you over and over: yes, it does! Your work in the household and parenting matters tremendously. It will echo into eternity.

But on the other hand, this is challenging because it reminds us of why parenting is so very, very hard. Parenting, seen properly, is an unceasing spiritual battle. A battle that God is using to refine us, and a battle that God will win for us, but if it feels like a fight to you, that's because it is.

When you are at home with children, you are in a spiritual realm that would make even the most zealous monastics jealous. One of the famous contemplative writers of the twentieth century, Carlo Carretto, spent years and years in the Sahara Desert, seeking God in a life of prayer and solitude. Later he admitted that he felt his mother, who spent thirty years raising children, was much more contemplative (and much less selfish!) than he was.[1] I don't find this surprising at all. As author Ruth Chou Simons so wonderfully puts it, "motherhood is sanctifying." I can only smile and add, so is fatherhood.

So in the end, reframing the household as the school of love where the most important spiritual work happens should be both challenging and comforting, because an implicit claim is that we don't have to retreat to the mountain tops or solitary edges of human experience to meet God and serve him. Rather, we find God and his mission at the center of loud families.[2]

---

1. Quoted in Ronald Rolheiser, *Domestic Monastery* (Brewster, MA: Paraclete Press, 2019).
2. For a fascinating and surprisingly beautiful book on seeking families as the place of spiritual formation, rather than seeking solitude and retreats, see Ernest Boyer Jr.,

Finally, all things spiritual must eventually become practical. So while I have tried to root the beginning of each chapter in good theology, I try to end each chapter where good theology is supposed to lead us—good practice.

At the end of each chapter, you will find the key habits summarized and pulled together on one page. This is not only so you can be reminded of them but also so you can find them easily as you (I hope) go back and try them out.

A Note on Age and Adaptation

One of the things that writing from the trenches means is that while the themes and the habits are applicable to children of all ages, my examples will naturally tend toward younger children. I will draw on childhood and my own coming of age to speak toward adolescents and teens, but most of my parenting experience is in the younger years. So while you will notice that, you will also notice that as the book progresses, I will acknowledge the movement of time and speak more and more to the aging of our children. By the time we get to the epilogue, we'll be imagining us all old together.

Another thing to note is that I write from a fairly traditional family. I am so grateful that Lauren and I have a strong marriage and healthy children, but I am also aware that many people— including some of my friends, colleagues, and neighbors—do not. I want to acknowledge that with compassion and empathy. Depending on where you are, you may read sections or habits wondering how this applies to your different family situation. I have decided that it is wiser to let you make that application than

Finding God at Home: Family Life as Spiritual Discipline (San Francisco: Harper and Row, 1984).

to imagine that I can do it for you. When you read the chapter on marriage, you may desperately wish you had one. Or when you read the chapter on play, you may painfully wish your child were healthy enough to romp around. I can affirm that, nonetheless, the Christian themes of covenant love (in marriage) and healthy imaginations (in play) are applicable to all of us broken people, no matter our broken family situations. But I will not be so presumptuous as to apply it to your situation; I will let you do so. So at the end of each chapter, you will see a note on adaptation, encouraging you to do just that.

But no matter the ages of our children or the structures of our families, we can all relate on one thing—our brokenness as parents. We are all in need of grace and love, and that, you will find, over and over, is the main theme.

So Remember, Love Is at the Root of Everything

"Love is at the root of everything—all learning, all parenting, all relationships—love or the lack of it. And what we hear or see on the screen is part of who we become."

I love this quote in part because it is from an unexpected source: Mr. Rogers, the TV personality who was better known for asking, "Won't you be my neighbor?" But as you may know, Fred Rogers was a seminary-educated minister and follower of Jesus who saw himself as a missionary to television.[3] And even more, as someone who felt called to minister to children, he was radically attuned to the redemptive power of habit in children's lives. (Unsurprising if you recall his famous way of taking off his jacket and shoes every single show.)

---

3. See the 2018 documentary on Fred Rogers by Morgan Neville, *Won't You Be My Neighbor?*

But mostly I love this quote by Fred Rogers because it reminds me, over and over, that the motivating concern for all this talk about habits and caring for children is love.

You will, inevitably, at times while reading this book be tempted to wonder, "Isn't this legalistic? Isn't it the power of God that changes us, not the power of our habits?" I will try to remind you that no, it is not legalistic. And yes, it is the power of God that changes us, habits included.

I will call your attention to this over and over not so much because I want to defend my stance but because it is opportunity to remind you over and over of the message of God's grace.

Caring about how habits are shaping your family is not legalistic. What would be legalistic is saying that God loves you more because of your habits. Or that you can earn your salvation by picking the right habits. You can't. And thank God, you don't need to!

The good news of Christianity is that Jesus' death on the cross has paid for all of our failures (including our bad parenting habits), and his resurrection from the grave is the promise of a new life (including new parenting habits). It is that work of God that saves us, by grace and through faith—not our works (of habits or otherwise).[4] That God died for us while we were still sinners is a demonstration of his great love,[5] and that love is why we care about habits.

So as I will remind you at the end of every chapter, our habits won't change God's love for us, but God's love for us can and should change our habits.

So in light of his grace and love, let us begin.

---

4. Eph. 2:8–10.
5. Rom. 5:8.

PART 2

HABITS OF THE
HOUSEHOLD

CHAPTER 1

WAKING

My eyes snap open as I hear the scream in the middle of the night. I am halfway to the bedroom door by the time my brain begins putting things together. It's coming from the boys' room. Probably Coulter. It's amazing what the mind can do before you know the mind is doing anything.

I am halfway down the hallway before he even takes a breath to start his second scream, and I open the door just in time to watch him let it rip.

He is sitting up in his little bed, looking every bit the tiny human that he is. His "big boy" bed is barely bigger than a park bench, and he is clutching his blankies. His hair is rumpled. The pacifier clipped onto the collar of his Spider-Man pj's dangles down his chest.

I gather him up into my arms. Like all kids in crisis, he must feel love before he can talk about it. In a moment the screaming stops. As he quiets, I say, "Coulter, what's wrong, buddy?" He looks at me, for a moment calm, and then bursts back into tears. "A monster!" He wails. "Getting me!" The next couple of minutes are exactly what you expect: I sit with him, as his sniffles die down. I tell him there is no monster, and that it was only a dream, but such things are only so effective. Why? Because whether we're big or little, we humans struggle to connect this gap between our heads and our hearts.

Shaking in his bed at three years old, Coulter is a picture of the human condition. Rationality, by itself, has never calmed a single fear in children or in parents. It is entirely possible to know that one thing is true but feel completely the opposite. He "knows" there are no monsters in the closet, but he shakes in his bed nonetheless. We "know" that God loves us and is working everything out for good, yet we shake in our anxieties nonetheless. For all of us, fully coming to terms with reality is a process that must involve feeling as much as knowing.

This is what stories are for—moving reality from the head to the heart. We must tell and retell the stories of reality to ourselves and our children, lest we continue to live in our bad dreams. So I tell him a story.

"Coulter, if a monster tried to come get you, you know what I would do?" "What?" he says, half nervous and half curious. "I would grab him by his monster tail and spin him around the room like this." I whirl my hand over my head. "Then, when he was so dizzy, I would let him go and toss him out the window like this!" I throw the invisible monster at the window. Coulter suppresses a giggle at the thought of it.

Then I ask him, "Will I always be here to protect you?" This is a question we have rehearsed, and he knows his line: "Yeah," he says. I hold him for another moment. As a truer version of reality begins to settle in, he finally lies back down.

Soon we are both back in bed. Before I fall asleep, the thought briefly crosses my mind: "I am much more like Coulter than I'd like to admit." It's true, for all of us, really.[1]

---

1. See Paul David Tripp's excellent book *Parenting: Fourteen Gospel Principles That*

Before we are parents of our kids, we are children. Most important, children of a heavenly father. Understanding how we are parented by that heavenly father changes everything about the way we parent our children.

Coulter had woken up to an alternate version of reality. It was not real, but it caused real fear. He needed a parent to hold him, calm him, and speak the true story of reality over him.

Most days, we need the same thing. Most days, we wake up to our own monsters, desperately in need of a heavenly parent to remind us the truth about reality—that we are loved by a good God, and because of him, everything is going to be okay.

Waking Up to Reality

One of the great questions of life is whether we are awake to reality as it actually is or we live in alternate realities that abound with lies. The stakes are high, for the truth of God's reality will always set us free, but lies, like monsters, will always enslave us to constant fear.[2]

As parents, we must begin an examination of the habits of the household by looking at our own habits because, after all, we become our habits and our kids become us. And this examination begins with the habits of waking.

Before you get nervous, know that I am not going to tell you that we all need to be waking up two hours earlier for extended silent meditation. This chapter is about waking up to reality, and if you are a parent like me, then the reality is you are probably not getting enough sleep as it is. So don't worry. I'm much more interested in how we wake, which is fundamentally a spiritual

---

Can Radically Change Your Family (Wheaton, IL: Crossway, 2016) for an expounding on this theme.
2. John 8:32: "Then you will know the truth, and the truth will set you free."

matter, rather than exactly when we wake, which is a matter that changes with age and stage. So consider, for a moment, the spirituality of waking.

Waking is an incredible thing. We have spent hours of our lives unconscious and vulnerable. Then we open our eyes and try to relocate ourselves in reality. Where are we? What time is it? What do we have to do today? What is going on in the world? Who are we today? How do we feel about ourselves? What are we worth?

Waking from sleep may be considered a given, but waking to reality is not. As with Coulter, a lot depends on the stories we listen to as we wake. The difference is, while his monsters uncontrollably barge into dreams, as adults, our monsters are much more practiced—the lies we believe are most often products of the habits we practice. Which story of reality do we habitually rehearse every morning? Is it setting us free? Or is it enslaving us to lies?

When the first thing I do in the morning is roll over, grab my phone, and begin scanning work emails, I wake to the monsters of performance. The story of reality is about what I can get accomplished today and whether I can justify my existence. When I begin the morning in social media, I wake to the monsters of comparison and envy. The story of reality is about the pictures of other people's lives and whether I can measure up. When I begin the morning in the news headlines, the monsters of fear and anger nearly jump through the screen. The story of reality is about how the world is falling apart and how mad I should be at the others who just don't get it. Or when I lie in bed recounting the day's to-do list (or when I jump up and immediately start the rush to get everyone out the door on time), I wake to the monster of busyness. The story of reality is how there is always too much to do and never enough time to do it.

All of these lies are like the monsters in Coulter's closet. Intellectually, I know that they aren't the real stories of the world.

But practically, it sure seems like they are because I rehearse feeling them every morning.

Habits of waking may be small and mostly unconscious, but they are never neutral—and that's why they are so powerful. The power of habits is their unique combination of spirituality and invisibility. They tell us stories about reality and lead us in patterns of worship, all while staying under the radar. Which is why the stakes of habits are high. What is at stake in our habits of waking is whether we practically believe the gospel of Jesus.

At best, the morning rituals of a household support the reality that God loves us and that his love is the defining fact of the universe. Here our habits of waking serve as gospel liturgies that push us into the arms of a father who loves us, and then send us out into the world to love others. But at worst, our habits of waking indulge alternative realities where the universe depends on us and what we do today. This is the gospel of humankind, where our rituals tell us that we have to keep up to survive and turn the household into a school of rush, fear, and frustration.

So we must wake up to how we wake up. We must see that the first role of a parent is not to get everyone up on time but to root our household habits of waking in the truth of the gospel. For in the story of God, our call is not simply to wake up our bodies each day but to awaken our hearts to God's love.

Waking Up in Light of the Story of God

"Let there be light."[3]

These are the famous first words of God in Scripture, kicking off the metaphor of light that will run through the whole of

3. Gen. 1:3.

the story. Light is what happens when God speaks in Genesis. Light is what surrounds things whenever God shows up to someone in the Old Testament. Light is what falls on the psalmist's path when God speaks his words. Light of the world is the central metaphor for who Jesus is. Light is what blinds Paul. Light is what lets him see again. Light is what Paul can't stop writing about in his letters, telling us to shine like stars and be children of light.[4] And, of course, light is where the Bible ends, with God himself lighting up the world. In the new heaven and the new earth, there will be no need for the sun in the sky because we will have the Son of God.

Like God, light always wins in the end. Where there is light, there can be no darkness. "This is why it is said: 'Wake up, sleeper, rise from the dead, and Christ will shine on you.'"[5]

If the light of morning is what wakes us to the day, then the light of Christ must be what wakes us to reality. It is the light of Christ that pulls back the curtains of the heart.

One of my favorite moments of morning is when Lauren comes downstairs, because her first task is to pull back the curtains. For whatever reason, I tend to default to just sitting on the couch in the dark of morning with coffee, reading, and journaling. Sometimes I am alone. Sometimes a boy who has woken early sits nearby. (Sometimes a boy who has woken early crawls all over me and scribbles on the page where I'm trying to journal.) But in any case, most often, none of us bothers to pull back the curtains and let the light in.

While the creaky floorboards and drafty walls are downsides of living in such an old house as ours, the nine-foot ceilings and tall windows are a bonus. So when Lauren comes down

---

4. Phil. 2:15; Eph. 5:8.
5. Eph. 5:14.

and inevitably begins opening curtains, the house dramatically changes. All at once there are windows to the world everywhere, and suddenly I see the world as it is. Sometimes the house is flooded with morning light. Other times I realize that the sun is not up yet. Sometimes I had no idea it was raining.

It always reminds me that our capacity to see the world as it is is not a given. Intellectually knowing it is morning is one thing; staring at the sunlit slant of rectangle across the rug is another. One engages the head, and the other engages the heart and the head.

What is true in the house is true in our spiritual life. We must find ways in the morning to pull back the curtains of our tired hearts and let the light in. And this is precisely what the spiritual disciplines are for.

Three Habits to Let the Light In

The best way to understand the spiritual disciplines as morning routines of the household is to imagine them as ways to let the light in.

While you might think of the spiritual disciplines as something extra to do, I would encourage you to think of them as something you are already doing—though you might not know it. Right now, you have a routine. You are going through some liturgy of morning, whether in your kitchen or on your phone, and it is reinforcing a story of the world that may or may not be true. This is a spiritual habit. All our mundane habits are. They disciple our hearts in certain directions.

Understanding that our habits are already discipling us helps us see the classic spiritual disciplines in their full dimensions. They don't just open our hearts to the reality of God's story, they also displace other habits that were leading us in liturgies of false stories.

Below are three examples of how the simple spiritual disciplines of Scripture and prayer can become short morning routines that help a family pull back the curtains of the heart.

Habit of Waking 1: Try a Short Kneeling Prayer at Your Bedside upon Waking

I usually wake to a head full of thoughts and questions. "Why is that kid up so early?" "What am I going to say at that meeting?" Or, "Why am I always so tired?" As we all do, I have an option each morning: Do I indulge this distorted reality, or do I bend the knee to God's reality?

The habit of kneeling by my bed to pray immediately upon waking helps me displace all these other possible thoughts and spend the first moment of morning looking for the light. Though I am tired, the act of kneeling takes hold of the mind by taking hold of the body. Though I am full of anxious thoughts about the day, saying a short prayer gently introduces a different reality: the backdrop of God's love and care for me despite what I need to do. Though many of my questions about the day are probably valid (our monsters always wear a mask of truth), framing them in a short prayer sets them in the context of God's concern for my concerns. It reminds me that my troubles do exist, though they might not mean what I think they mean. My concerns are not to be ignored but rather examined in the light of the reality of God's love.

As I have practiced this over the years,[6] I find I often rely on a couple of one-sentence memorized prayers (a few are included at the end of this chapter for examples). But just as often, I simply put my first thoughts into the form of a prayer.

---

6. See chapter 1 of *The Common Rule: Habits of Purpose for an Age of Distraction* for the story on how this practice came to be a keystone habit.

If I wake up to exhaustion, I might put it into a request: "Lord, don't let me snap at the kids just because I chose to go to bed late."

If my work concerns clutter my mind, they will probably find their way into a petition: "God, may I reflect your image in my work today and not worry about my own image."

If I'm struggling with my annoyances with my kids (which always threatens to reduce them to problems to be managed instead of image-bearers to be loved), I will try to put that into a prayer where they become human again: "Lord, may I love and serve my children this morning as you loved and served me."

Usually this short habit is carried out alone and right beside the bed, immediately after shutting off the alarm. Sometimes it happens with Lauren and it gets drawn out a bit because it's Saturday. Once in a while it happens with a kid at my side because they have woken me early. If so, I will invite them into the ritual by putting an arm around their shoulder and asking them to kneel with me. Sometimes they want to pray too; usually they just want to hear me do it.

But no matter how it unfolds, this moment is always as short as it is significant.

"Give me a place to stand . . . and I will move the world," Archimedes said of the power of the lever. It's true. Small things in the right place have enormous consequences.

So it is with prayer. The power of prayer is not proportionate to its length, for prayer works outside the physics of our intentions. And that is a good thing. No matter how short, prayer is the lever that can lift the heaviest of hearts. Lift them up to see reality as it really is—that we are children of the King, that today he is redeeming all things, and that we are invited into that glorious reality.

You should know, of course, that this is not a quick fix to

make life painless. Nothing is. None of the spiritual disciplines promise to make our life simple or give us eternal patience with our children. None of them will banish our worries and exhaustions forever at the snap of a finger.

But what they can do is open our hearts to see that God has been there all along, waiting patiently to meet us right in the midst of our complexities and anxieties. And in the light of God's presence with us, we are reminded that the monsters we feared never existed after all.

Remember, it didn't help Coulter when I just told him the monsters weren't real. What helped is when I sat with him and held him. God offers this to us, morning after morning. He is the one sitting at our bedside, putting an arm around our tired body, inviting us to join him in prayer.

Habit of Waking 2: Make a Habit of Looking to the Scriptures before Looking at Your Smartphone

Neurologists say that we are all born looking for someone who is looking for us.[7] It's a beautiful way of describing what happens when the gaze of a newborn meets the gaze of a mother. Interpersonal neurobiology suggests that this moment is indeed as staggering as we feel it is. In this moment, two brains are changing each other. No matter the trauma of birth, in this first

---

7. I am indebted to Curt Thompson not only for this idea but for my general understanding of how the modern insights of interpersonal neurobiology intertwine with Christian spirituality. You will notice an undercurrent of brain science and neurology running through this book. I do not try to footnote each sentence, but in general my understanding of neurology and child development has come through *The Whole-Brain Child* and some other books by Daniel J. Siegel. These books are extremely useful but are best read through Curt Thompson's Christian lens of the soul. See his books *Anatomy of the Soul: Surprising Connections between Neuroscience and Spiritual Practices That Can Transform Your Life and Relationships* (Carol Stream, IL: Tyndale, 2010) and *The Soul of Shame: Retelling the Stories We Believe about Ourselves* (Downers Grove, IL: InterVarsity Press, 2015).

look, both of them feel the same: *here is the one I've been looking for*. In their gaze the world will be okay. It is an awe-inspiring moment that we never really get over.

I would suggest that we all go through the rest of our lives in different iterations of this moment, and the morning is one such repeating pattern.

Each morning we are born anew into the world, and each morning we wake up looking for someone who is looking for us. We are hungry for the gaze of someone who loves us. We will look for it everywhere and anywhere, trying to find something to fill that God-shaped (and God-sized) hole our hearts.

This is what we are doing when we turn our gaze to the screen first thing in the morning. The human condition is to be uncertain about our identity. And because we are not sure who we are, when we look at emails or social media, our tired hearts cannot help but look to see if there is something there to fill that void. This is why we can so easily turn responding to work emails into ways to justify our sense of self-worth, or turn scrolling social media into liturgies of comparison. We are looking for someone who is looking for us. The problem is, we will never find that in the screen.

Facial recognition software is one of the most spiritually revealing technologies to come our way. All we have to do is turn our gaze to our screen and like the face of a mother, it lights up at our mere attention. Yet, strangely and somewhat tragically, there is no gaze to be returned. There is only the strange blue glow of our own fractured reflections. And these can become the monsters that haunt us.

We see the strange half-reflections of our own fears in the morning news. We see the hazy visions of who we wish we were as we scroll social media. We see refractions of our ambitions and worries in work emails and task lists. The tragedy, of course, is that we are looking for someone to look back at us, and no one is there. No wonder our hearts begin to flit with fear. No wonder our fingers begin to twitch with nervousness. Maybe if I scroll faster and farther, I will find something to calm the inner sense that everything is not okay. But at the bottom of the infinite feed is only more feed, the temptation to flick one more time. The heart turns down a final alley, only to find another alley. Isn't it strange to consider there is no bottom? It only goes on and on. No wonder our hearts get lost.

What we need, of course, is a parent. Someone to take the phone gently from our hands and tell us that social media was never intended to meet our infinite desires—on the contrary, it is programmed to profit off them. Like the promise of a liar or the worst lover, it just stretches your heart as far as it can. You were bound to break, which is why you have. It's a bad love story. And we all need to get out of it.

One of the best ways to do that is to cultivate the morning ritual of ignoring your phone until after you have found the gaze of God in Scripture.

Going to Scripture before we go to our smartphones is another small way to pattern the morning in the reality of God's love. But given the black-hole allure of the smartphone, it is probably one of the most radical habits of the household you can cling to. In turning our gaze to Scripture, we turn our gaze to the face of God, and find him looking back at us.

In a house full of children, this will look as messy as everything else does. Ideally, the pattern of Scripture before smartphone means I'm up before them, having a few minutes to read and reflect before they wake. But of course that is not always the reality, and it is important to know that that is fine. Sometimes, that is even better, because one of the ways we teach the habits of the household is by letting children observe our habits and inviting them into them. Some mornings this looks like listening to a psalm while holding a kid who is holding a sippy cup of milk on my lap.[8] He is invited into the routine. Occasionally it means reading a Bible story out loud to one of them. Many, many mornings it means they also get a book, or a coloring page, and we have some minutes of quiet before we start breakfast.

Sometimes I am tempted to think, "Does this really matter?" While it is totally understandable to wonder this, it is even more important to note that this seed of doubt—if given into—can become the crack in the foundation of the strongest routines. So in theory, I wonder over this, but in practice, I know the answer: "Yes. It is always the smallest routines that build the strongest foundations."

The Word of God is actually true and God's promises about it are actually real. It does not come back void. It pierces the heart. It reveals. Reading the Scriptures is a command *and* an invitation for a reason—it changes us. Further, as it turns out, habits are formative, patterns program us, and routines are liturgies. Making a ritual out of giving your attention to Scripture in the morning means a thousand other things you did not think about or intend: It means that your smartphone is not there distracting your brain with dopamine rushes. It means that taking a moment of pause is normal for your pace of life. It means you are slowly going through the Scriptures and starting to learn them. It means you are aggregating mornings where you do what you said you were going to do, honoring your conscience and casting

---

8. Is it ironic that I listen to Scripture on my phone while ignoring my phone? At first, but not really. Redeeming our use of technology is much less about banishing it than cultivating the patterns of using it well.

a small vote of habit in favor of becoming the kind of person you are called to become.[9]

So it is that the small things are the big things, and the tiny routines run the deepest.

But above all of that, we are unlocking something else with our gaze. By turning our face to the Scriptures, we look and find a God who is looking back. We find the parent we want to imitate. Above all, we go to Scripture because we want to become more like him, and in turn, our children, who are by default becoming more like us, become more like him too.

Habit of Waking 3: Practice a Short Moment of Gathering and Sending the Family

Schedules shape us. Usually the best way to realize this is looking at what happens when they are gone.

In 2020, when the Covid-19 pandemic unexpectedly brought all of our routines to a grinding halt, many of us found ourselves without a schedule. For a brief moment, this was freeing. Suddenly we didn't have to be anywhere at a certain time—but the reality soon set in. I still had to work, and the kids still had to learn, but with no morning meetings and no school bells ringing, we fell into this shapeless void of morning. I struggled to find the line between when to stop breakfast and start work. Without the drive to school, the kids had no moment that shifted them from free time to learning time.

Quickly, Lauren and I realized that we needed to build a

---

9. It is fascinating to note that popular writers on the psychology of habit note exactly the same thing that the tradition of Christian teaching on spiritual disciplines do: that our inner identity is deeply tied to our outer habits. James Clear, in his book *Atomic Habits* (New York: Avery, 2018), notes this aggregating power of small things and claims that ultimately habits make us who we are. He writes, "Every action you take is a vote for the type of person you wish to become. . . . Quite literally, you become your habits."

new schedule, not just to give shape to morning but to give it meaning too. One thing we—almost accidentally—began was a brief time of morning prayer together.

It began as a way to start the school day at home, gathering the kids at the table to say prayer before virtual school started. As this became a routine for their school day at home, Lauren asked one morning if I wanted to join, and I figured I could wait two more minutes to get to work, so why not stick around for it?

So we started gathering in the kitchen or maybe by the front door and Lauren would lead us through a short prayer. This was, as you might imagine, not without mishaps. Holding hands while standing in a circle seemed to be an irresistible temptation for the little ones to see if they could pull the older ones over. Which was in turn an invitation for the older ones to show the little ones that two could play at that game. Often, one or two little ones thought standing in a circle meant we were preparing for a round of ring-around-the-rosy. (You can imagine their disappointment when they realized it was just for prayer.)

And of course there was also a lot of shrugging of shoulders and "Do we have to do this?" But such are the perils of routines. Whether you are trying to get everyone to eat their veggies or buckle their seat belts, the most important habits will always be the source of questions and complaints—but parents persevere. Remember—that's why we're here.

As it slowly became a habit, things became more normal. Once we have all joined hands and (at least relative) quiet has descended, Lauren will say something like these words: "Father, Son, and Holy Spirit, thank you for this day." And we will all repeat it. Then she will say, "Bless us as we work, study, and play." And we say it too. She goes on: "Be present with us, and in all we do, may we bring glory and honor to you." And we follow along.

Sometimes the boys enthusiastically repeat after her; sometimes they drag their feet like prisoners to their execution. But every time, there is a brief moment when the family gathers to be sent out in prayer.

As this new pattern began to set in, almost immediately, I realized that something else was happening. Our joining together was marking the moment between when breakfast and dressing and preparation had ended, and the day of work and learning and serving was beginning. We had this before, but previously it was the frenzied call for everyone to "get in the car" or "get to the bus." Now prayer was transitioning us, and Lauren and I both began to feel the way this new schedule was shaping us.

After a while, I began to notice that previously the monster of "being on time" had haunted us and driven most of the details of our morning routine. In fact, I remember that for Whit's first few months of kindergarten, he would ask every morning in the car whether we were late. He seemed actually worried about it. Eventually I realized he was doing what kids do—adopting his parents' fears and internalizing a version of them all his own. The household scramble had implicitly taught him that morning was a time to rush and worry whether one of us was making the rest of us late.

There is still much to do and many places to be. That hasn't changed and likely never will. But morning prayer has changed the way we experience it. It has come to serve as a different way to pattern ourselves toward the day. Now the routine has taken the moment of rush and hurry and displaced it with a moment of prayer—we are sent into the day on purpose. We don't rush into the day simply because we have to.

Whether morning prayer or something else, a moment of gathering and sending can serve as a powerful reminder for parents and children that we not only begin the day in God's love, we are sent out to love. This is a reflection of the movement of the church. We come together in order to be sent out. This is how we imitate the missional movement of the body of Christ; the Lord draws us near to send us far.

This kind of movement can be imitated and varied in many ways: It could be a family breakfast and devotions, as I remember from my childhood. It could be a prayer you say during the car ride each morning. While it could be many things, I believe it is important to pay attention to this movement of gathering and sending, because without it, we usually default to being frayed and scattered by rush, rather than gathered and sent in love.

Habits as Grooves of Grace

Being able to see reality as it is is no small thing. It is not a given. Certainly not in one of the most difficult phases of life, which is parenting. There is no tiredness like the tiredness of a parent. And that is not just a physical reality, it is a spiritual one, which is why we parents desperately need habits that help pull the curtains back and wake our sleepy hearts to the light of Jesus.

Parenting cries out for a way to see. A way to see the significance of the moments that are passing before us, and a way to steward our families by stewarding those moments. No one has this clarity of sight or alertness of mind day after day to see reality as it is—which is why we need these habits. We don't cling to habits to show how good we are at this thing called parenting, we cling to habits because we know we are otherwise so bad at it.

As the grooves of grace called the spiritual disciplines become habits, they take moments where we would otherwise be tired failures and guide us toward God's strength and love. This is, of course, the hallmark of God's grace: it meets us in weakness and protects us from ourselves. And this is exactly what a parent needs, morning after morning after morning.

HABITS OF WAKING
FORMING PARENTS

Main Idea

Waking up is a spiritual reality as much as it is a physical one. We cannot be good parents of children until we are children of God. Spiritual disciplines help us pull back the curtains and see reality as it actually is. The goal is to awaken to the reality of God's love for us and be sent out to parent in that reality.

> **Remember,** you already have some kind of spiritual discipline that starts your morning. Consider those habits and whether they are discipling you in love or rush, in grace or anxiety.

Scripture before Phone

Along with your spouse, commit to a set of practices that make a habit of ignoring your phone in the morning and going to Scripture instead.

Tips to start:

- Set your phone to Do Not Disturb so you don't see notifications upon waking; perhaps also set an alarm or change the wallpaper on your phone to remind you.
- Try going to the same couch or chair each morning and placing your Bible and journal in a place nearby.
- Try following a reading plan or a devotional, ideally with your spouse or others.
- Be comfortable with brief readings and prayers as the norm, but let the habit grow to longer times as permitted on weekends or slower days.

- Consider leaning toward print Bibles, but when you do use a Scripture app, use voice activation to open it so you don't get distracted with other things on your phone as you open it.
- When just beginning, tell a friend or spouse that you are trying to develop this habit so they can help keep you accountable. Ideally try thirty days together.
- Explore practices like *Lectio Divina* to help guide you through meaningful prayer or meditation when you're short on time.
- Don't get mad when you mess up. Habits are norms, not rules, and grace is real, not theoretical.

> *"Waking from sleep may be considered a given, but waking to reality is not."*

Ideas for Morning Kneeling Prayers

Briefly, and beside the bed:

- Lord, thank you for the gift of another day. Help me walk with your love into whatever work you have called me to today. Amen.
- Lord, thank you for the gift of a day with the ones you have given me to love. Be among us as we work at play and work at love. Amen.
- Lord, please help. Remind me of your power in my weakness as I try to love others, despite my exhaustion. Amen.

Remember, you don't have to try everything at once. One small change can have big spiritual impact. Pick one thing to start.

Further Resources

*The Common Rule: Habits of Purpose for an Age of
    Distraction,* Justin Whitmel Earley
The Book of Common Prayer
Revised Common Lectionary
Every Moment Holy, Douglas Kaine McKelvey
*God's Wisdom for Navigating Life: A Year of Daily Devotions
    in the Book of Proverbs,* Timothy Keller with Kathy Keller

A Gathering and Sending Prayer

*Try gathering the family sometime before everyone is about
to leave, joining hands, and saying a quick prayer together.
A parent can say each phrase, and the children can repeat
it. Make sure to keep the phrases short in words and simple
in language.*

- **Father, Son, and Holy Spirit**, thank you for this day.
- **Bless us** as we work, study, and play.
- **Be present with us** in all we do.
- May we bring **glory** and **honor** to you. **Amen.**

A Note on Adapting

Your job or life stage may mean that your morning looks
quite different. But as a general rule, see where you can
avoid screens and rush and instead embrace a short spiritual discipline.

> **We Always Need the Reminder of Grace:** God's love in-
> spires our action, but our action does not inspire God's
> love. Our family habits will not change God's love for us,
> but God's love for us should change our family habits.

CHAPTER 2

MEALTIMES

One fall shortly after our fourth son was born, Lauren and I decided we should do a mini vacation in the mountains of Virginia. A friend had offered us a free cabin at the base of the Appalachians, and somehow the allure of a cheap fall getaway weekend overshadowed the reality of "vacationing" with a newborn. A vacation with young children is really just going somewhere scenic and working overtime shifts of parenting hours. Great memories for the kids, but hard work for you. This fit the description perfectly.

It was that Saturday morning, sitting in a restaurant with large windows at the base of the mountains, that things started to go very south. Bringing any child to a restaurant is always playing a game of chicken with chance, and we had brought four—one of whom was an infant. The odds were not in our favor, and it showed, particularly on the face of our waitress. It appeared from her pursed lips that she did not think our kids were nearly as cute as we do, nor was she impressed that we were attempting this herculean feat. Frankly, she looked like she just did not want to deal with all of us on this particular Saturday morning. Incidentally, neither did I. But there we were. So we dug in.

She hadn't even brought out the menus and already one boy had chased another around the table and *multiple* pieces of silverware had been dropped (spiked?) on the floor—as if trying to emphasize the fact that this modern, mountain-chic restaurant with bare concrete floors and large wooden rafters seemed to be specifically designed to amplify and echo kid noise. Amid the chaos, Lauren sat at the other end of the table nursing our newborn, Shep, and gave me that smile that cheerfully said, "What do you expect me to do? I'm busy." So I was on.

Being way too prideful to admit defeat, pick up some bad donuts from a gas station, and return back to our free cabin with our sense of dignity, I used the loud, deep voice thing instead to try to command attention: "Boys! Settle down!" It worked for a moment, until I remembered that this restaurant was designed to echo. Embarrassed, I shifted tactics.

"New game!" I said. "Game?" they repeated in unison. I'd gotten their attention now, but I didn't have an idea yet. "Yes! Game. It's called the . . ." I scanned the table; the nearest thing was pepper. "The pepper game!"

"The pepper game!" they all chirped. The echoes brought it back a few times.

"Now, the way you play the pepper game is only one person holds the pepper. And what's very important is you *cannot talk* unless you have the pepper." A knowing shadow crossed their faces—they are not amused by "no talking" games. "But!" I interjected quickly, "When you *do* have the pepper, you *have to* talk. And you have to answer a question. So the first question is . . . favorite dessert!" Before they had time to object, I placed it in front of Ash. "Ash, you start!"

We went around the table, and everyone did a dessert. Then Whit started. He picked favorite movies. We went through animals, cousins, cereals, Ninja Turtles, and more before the pancakes arrived, and in the end, breakfast was salvaged. Barely.

It still contained many antics and the obligatory I'm-really-sorry-about-all-that tip. But somewhere between the spilled syrup and dropped sausages there was a rhythm of passing the pepper and answering questions.

I have gone over and over that morning in my mind since then. A semblance of conversation stood like a small guardrail between us and total chaos. It was only a small pattern of conversation, and one that had to be practiced and learned through a child-friendly game, but it changed things. On a deeper level, I thought about my extended family and the loud and crowded tables that make life so rich. It struck me that the difference between people who happen to live together and families who befriend each other are rhythms of conversation at mealtimes.

Food and Conversation in the Story of God

In the story of God, eating is not just some daily routine of cramming food that allows us to survive, it is a ritual of communing with others that allows us to thrive.

It's remarkable how much the Bible talks about food as a spiritual matter. Sometimes food in the Bible shows us that God is a faithful provider.[1] Sometimes it shows us that God is a generous host.[2] Sometimes it teaches us about our hunger for something more.[3] Sometimes it tells us what communing with God will

---

1. Gen. 1:29–31 and 9:1–5.
2. Ps. 23:5: "You prepare a table before me . . ."
3. Matt. 4:4: "Man shall not live on bread alone, but on every word that comes from the mouth of God."

be like.[4] But rarely is food just about physical nourishment; it is always about driving us toward relationship with God and others.

For the family, seeing the role of food in the story of God means that we see food in terms of its end goal—*relationship*. That means that the family that wants to become friends needs to take rhythms of food and conversation seriously.

But the idea that patterns of conversation at mealtimes are keystone habits of the household presupposes something much more fundamental—that you eat together in the first place.

Coming to the Table as a Keystone Spiritual Habit of the Family

It is not a given that a family eats together at all, yet one of the most loving things you can do for your family is simply to sit down, at the same time, in the same place, and eat together.

This is well-studied wisdom. Numerous studies have linked family meals to all sorts of positive family outcomes, from better academics to better behavior and reduced drug and alcohol abuse.[5] I have also heard that the thing that most Rhodes Scholars have in common was that their families ate together. But this is not just a matter of resumes and academics, the effects of regular meals are deeply spiritual. For example, Don Everts and the Barna Group found in their study of Christian households that

---

4. John 6:35: "Then Jesus declared, 'I am the bread of life. Whoever comes to me will never go hungry, and whoever believes in me will never be thirsty.'"

5. See, for example, Marla E. Eisenberg et al., "Correlations between Family Meals and Psychosocial Well-Being among Adolescents," *Archives of Pediatrics and Adolescent Medicine* 158, no. 8 (August 2004): 792–96; Marla E. Eisenberg et al., "Family Meals and Substance Use: Is There a Long-Term Protective Association?" *Journal of Adolescent Health* 43, no. 2 (August 2008): 151–56; Bisakha Sen, "The Relationship between Frequency of Family Dinner and Adolescent Problem Behaviors after Adjusting for Other Family Characteristics," *Journal of Adolescence* 33, no. 1 (February 2010): 187–96.

the families who were "spiritually vibrant" shared one amazing thing in common—they had loud tables.[6]

To understand why a rhythm as simple as coming to the table could be so significant across so many areas, we have to understand the idea of a keystone habit.

A keystone habit is one that supports a lot of other good habits. Exercise is a classic example. Studies consistently find that participants who were asked to exercise, even as little as once a week, without prompting started to eat better, sleep more, smoke less, and so on.[7] Apparently, it is simply a human phenomenon that when we commit to certain smaller rhythms, a lot of other rhythms fall into place.

This is fundamental wisdom for parents. It means that we parents who want to pattern our households in gospel formation should not just be looking for that one-off spiritual conversation that we hope our kids remember, we should be patterning our houses with the kinds of keystone family rhythms that turn kids into disciples of Jesus.

Coming to the table to talk is one such keystone habit.

To visualize this significance, consider a family dinner through the practical lens compared to the liturgical lens.

Seeing Family Habits through the Liturgical Lens

I do not want to over-romanticize that idea that sitting down to talk with children is at all easy (or even pleasant). On many days, it is very hard, quite a mess, and frankly, a logistical nightmare.

---

6. Don Everts, *The Spiritually Vibrant Home: The Power of Messy Prayers, Loud Tables, and Open Doors* (Downers Grove, IL: InterVarsity Press, 2020). Note they also found that those families also had habits of hospitality and prayer—topics we will pick up on in later chapters.

7. Charles Duhigg, *The Power of Habit: Why We Do What We Do in Life and Business* (New York: Random House, 2012), 108-9.

But just as morning routines help us pull back the curtains and see reality as it actually is, so do many other habits of the household reveal the nature of spiritual worship that is happening in the most ordinary habits of the household.

I will call that the "liturgical lens." Put simply, the liturgical lens is the idea of having the eyes to see the spiritual worship bound up in a habit we didn't think was spiritual at all.[8]

Family Dinner through the Practical Lens

One might guess that a family dinner begins with sitting down. Not at all. Like a river, there are all kinds of flowing tributaries upstream that need to come together to make this happen. Before anything happens, Lauren has undertaken the unending work of grocery buying and borne the constant mental load of meal planning. I have rushed home from work even though there were four emails I was supposed to send by close of business (which will now be tasks for after the kids' bedtime).

I get home and am greeted by the typical tackles and punches that are the boys' standard welcome. At this point, Lauren has said one thousand "not yets" to the ravaging pack of children who have begged and pleaded for yet another snack before dinner, yet as we begin to herd said pack to the table, suddenly three out of four of them have an epiphany of something else they want to do and scatter. We ring the dinner bell again, pull one out from behind a couch, pry toys out of hands, shout threats up the stairwell, and so on.

Once finally seated, I get the matches out to light our candle,

---

8. For a worthwhile deeper dive on the idea of seeing with a liturgical lens, see James K. A. Smith's work in the three books *Desiring the Kingdom: Worship, Worldview, and Cultural Formation* (Grand Rapids, MI: Baker Academic, 2009), *Imagining the Kingdom: How Worship Works* (Grand Rapids, MI: Baker Academic, 2013), and *Awaiting the King: Reforming Public Theology* (Grand Rapids, MI: Baker Academic, 2017). I am indebted to his work for my understanding of the liturgical nature of habits.

our little ritual that signals the beginning of dinner. Fight one breaks out over who will light it. I declare that I alone will light it. Groans wash in like the tide. I light the candle as we all say, "Christ is light." Fight two breaks out over who will blow out the match. I declare that the littlest—Shep—will get to do it. Groans wash back in.

"Let's pray," I say. We take hands. "Jesus, we thank—"

"Stop, Ash!" Coulter yells. Ash looks baffled. "He's holding my hand wrong!" Coulter cries.

"Okay, let's just do it right," I say through gritted teeth.

No sooner have we all chorused "Amen" than the fear sets in. Every male at the table including me (meaning everyone at the table except Lauren, God bless her) begins to worry that they won't get enough food and starts grabbing for things. As we begin to eat, Coulter mentions that he hates sweet potatoes. We have a table-wide reminder about how we don't talk about things we don't like at the table, we only talk about the things we do like.

Lauren asks Whit what his "rose and thorn" of the day were—our parlance for a high and low of the day. Whit begins to answer, but Ash accidentally spills the water.

"That's okay, just clean it up," Lauren and I say in tired, rote unison.

Ash spreads the water around the table with a towel as Whit shares about some LEGO creations he built, and Coulter chimes in with an extended monologue on his rose, which was fighting with his cousin. (Apparently he enjoyed it.)

"What was your rose, Mama?" I ask Lauren, but I'm cut off because Shep suddenly spikes his bowl on the table in a signal that he's done. There is an impressive shower of food bits at his corner of the table. He gets scolded, then excused to go play—Ash wants to join but we remind him he hasn't shared about his day yet.

With Shep playing across the room, we finally get a few words in. Lauren shares about an email she got on one of her consulting projects and for two or three minutes, we approximate what might be considered conversation. And that's all, because then it's time to clean. Ash protests—"We have to clean again!?"

Lauren sweeps the two littles toward the bath as I assign the older two tasks, which they perform with varying degrees of success.

Forty-five minutes later, here we are—half exhausted and left to clean up the results of their "cleaning up," only so we can repeat the whole thing tomorrow. One might wonder, why put yourself through the ringer like that, night after night?

But while the normal happens, other things happen too, and it is worth pulling back the metaphorical curtains now and seeing it through the liturgical lens.

Family Dinner through the Liturgical Lens

First, note that family dinner is not in any sense practical. It's far more efficient for us to each have a microwave dinner on our own varied schedules. But the tributaries of planning that lead to this moment of family dinner signal something—that communing, not consuming, is the household's center of gravity. So we sync our schedules, even when it is not easy. Extracurriculars, sports, happy hours, and late meetings will always try to compete, but none of those are our center of gravity. The family cannot revolve around these things; these things must revolve around the family.

When we light a candle, mental attention is called by physical attention. We all look at the same tiny explosion of a match. We smell the smoke, watch it burn. As it turns out, kids like fire. Fire signals that something is happening here. Indeed it is. The most ordinary and sacred of traditions is unfolding: family dinner is beginning.

"Christ is light!" we proclaim, setting the candle in the midst of the table. Sure, the profundity of the statement is mostly lost in the chaos. But these things are not about the one moment, they are about aggregating moments that become new normals. I now cannot see a candle lit without hearing an echo of children saying "Christ is light" in my head. They are like little theological stones we carry around in our pockets, turning them over in our palms in spare moments.

When we take hands, we are reminded that human touch is significant. Bodies are finicky. So are hearts. We practice reaching out to each other in ways that honor each other and symbolize our unity.

Then we pray. This is one of the number of times the family will say a prayer together throughout the day. In the words of the prayer, we are reminded that gratitude is the heartbeat of our communal life. Why do we get food when so many struggle? Why is the table full of things that died just so we could live? Why did Christ die just so that we could live? These sacramental mysteries hover around us on a regular Tuesday night.

In the passing of dishes we practice delayed gratification. In complimenting the meal, we practice the power of spoken encouragement. In withholding criticisms, we practice the virtue of silence, we are reminded that lots of things we think aren't worth saying. In roses and thorns and questions and pepper games, we practice telling stories, recalling memories, celebrating and sympathizing with each other.[9] We practice forgiving when someone spills something (again!). And in waiting until

---

9. Note that going through "roses and thorns" and "highs and lows" with children has an echo of the examen, the classic spiritual discipline of meditating on a day and asking where the Lord was present or where you felt he was absent. Habits that may seem inane actually till important soil in the hearts of our children. See more on the practice of examen in Adele Calhoun's *Spiritual Disciplines Handbook: Practices That Transform Us* (Downers Grove, IL: InterVarsity Press, 2015).

we're excused, we practice sticking around even when we don't want to—the root of learning loyalty.

Finally, as we help clean and reset the kitchen for the next day, we practice the truth that the gift of communal life takes the ethic of communal labor. We grow accustomed to the rhythms of work it takes to produce the relationships we desperately need.

Behold, then, the way a noisy dinner table echoes with the gospel. Light from darkness, and prayers from the mouths of babes. Forgiveness and gratefulness, reconciliation and discipline. But none of it sanctimonious. And all of it real liturgy.

Why Seeing the Household through the Lens of Liturgy Is So Important

This book began with a claim that the most significant thing about any household is what is considered normal. Why is this so important? Because the normal is what shapes us the most, though we notice it the least. It is precisely the unremarkable nature of the normal that gives it such remarkable power. All of our unspoken values get hidden under the invisibility cloak of the ordinary. We think of our day-to-day routines as neutral simply because we see them so often.

But putting on the liturgical lens allows us to lift that cloak and see what is happening when we don't think anything is happening. The liturgical lens allows us to see all of our normal moments for what they really are: moments of worship to someone or something. This pushes us to ask, "What exactly are we worshiping when we suppose we're not worshiping anything at all?"

Understanding that family habits are family liturgies clarifies where the work of worship and spiritual formation are actually happening—*in the normal.* For the most part, the place for this work is not in the moments we set aside as "spiritual." It is rather in the messy day-to-day patterns that the real work of spiritually formative parenting is done.

To me, this is freeing. I used to think I needed get the day-to-day stuff done and out of the way to get to the real spiritual work of parenting—some special conversation where the magic would really happen. But now I see that the magic of God's grace abounds in the places I need it most: in the normal routines.

But this is also challenging because it suggests that we need to be comfortable with the mess if we're going to be serious about spiritual formation. The fact is, in family, if you're adverse to messy prayers, then you're adverse to prayer. If you can't tolerate spills, you'll avoid eating with kids. If you don't like conflict in relationship, then you're not going to like relationship. If you can't handle a mess in the kitchen, you can't handle hospitality. If you can't stomach awkward moments, you won't much like the conversation that leads to the great moments. And if you have trouble with fights, then you won't be much good at forgiveness.

Seeing with the liturgical lens expands our field of vision to see that the spiritually significant work of the household is not happening in spite of the mess but because of it. It also expands our field of vision to see that the work of the family is about more than the family. The family may be the beginning of our parental mission, but it is not the end of it. We cannot talk about the value of household meals without talking about the natural end of such meals—hospitality. But before we go there, let me make a brief note on the word *household*.

On Hospitality: The Household Is More Than the Nuclear Family

By this point, you may have noticed my preference for using the word household instead of family or house or another term.

There is an important reason for this: the biblical concept of the household is far more than the Western concept of the nuclear family. Just as the liturgical lens allows us to expand our vision of where God is at work, so thinking in terms of the household, instead of just the family unit, encourages us to think bigger about how God is working through our families.

The biblical idea of the household enlarges family both in dimension and direction. In terms of dimension, the biblical concept of the household is simply larger. It included extended family, as well as people who were economically connected to your family—workers or neighbors on the same land, and so on.[10] But in terms of direction, the biblical concept of the household also pushes back on the idea of "family first."[11] We don't care for our household because our responsibility is to our bloodline and no one else—that is a cloaked form of tribalism. Rather, we care for the family because it is through the household that God's blessing to us is extended to others.

The biblical direction of blessing is always outward, not inward. We are blessed in order to bless others.[12] This ethic will run throughout all the habits of the household we discuss in this book, but there is no better place to begin than at the table, for the table is a place where we turn strangers into friends.

Earlier, I noted Don Everts' writing about the Barna research demonstrating that messy tables are central to a spiritually vibrant family. As it turns out, so are open doors—or more specifically, the practice of inviting the stranger in.

---

10. Everts, The Spiritually Vibrant Home, 43–56.

11. See the excellent chapter "Family Is Not First," chapter 4 in Russell Moore, The Storm-Tossed Family: How the Cross Reshapes the Home (Nashville: Broadman and Holman, 2018).

12. Gen. 12:2: "I will make you into a great nation, and I will bless you; I will make your name great, and you will be a blessing."

Ordinary Hospitality Is Radical Hospitality

A few years ago, our good friend Drew asked if there was any way he could be more involved in our family. Drew was single and in his thirties and didn't have any family in town. While I appreciated his question, I never really followed up on it because, well, with a bunch of young kids, hospitality is a really daunting task.

A few months later, Drew persisted and brought it up again.

"I mean, we'd love to have you over for dinner," I said, "but I'm not sure you'd like it. You realize our family dinners are crazy, right? Like you might get punched or sprayed with food."

"Hospitality is not entertaining," he helpfully reminded me. "I just want to be part of a normal family rhythm."

On the one hand, I worried he didn't know what he was getting himself into, but on the other, his words were convicting. The reason I hadn't taken him up on the idea to join in our family rhythm was because—well, I felt I needed to clean it up before I let anyone in. I liked the *idea* of him and others coming by, but any night in particular seemed way too messy and hectic.

But Drew's words helped me realize that I was indeed mixing up entertainment and hospitality. Entertaining guests is when you clean everything, make up nice plates of food and batches of drinks, and maybe get a sitter for the kids. At best, entertaining is where we honor our guests by offering an experience of comfort and beauty. At worst, entertaining is where we honor ourselves by showing off what we can pull off.

In any case, hospitality is different. Hospitality is simply opening the door. Hospitality is welcoming someone into the unvarnished mess. It is inviting someone into the chaos because that's where real family happens. I see now that my desire to entertain Drew rather than be hospitable to him was ironically a way of keeping him at arm's length from the family. Wanting things to be perfect often means that nothing happens at all.

Now, years later, Thursday nights are dinners with Drew. It is the day with plans we don't need to confirm ahead of time. It is the day where it is normal for me to get home from work and find Drew trying to help manage a temper tantrum while Lauren tends something on the stove, or vice versa, I'll find Drew cooking something at the stove while Lauren chases a boy around. The house looks the same. It's a mess. The only difference is that Uncle Drew is in it, and that's what they call him now. And if there's a Little League game on Thursday night and we don't have dinner, then Uncle Drew is there to watch from the third-base line.

To Drew, I'm sure the image of our cluttered counters, half-cleaned spills on the floor, dried food on the baby chair, and so on are normal. I imagine that's just what he thinks our house looks like—and he would be right. It does. And many of my images of Drew now are from the back deck, while I watch him jump with my kids on the trampoline, or romp with Shep on the living room rug, or play checkers with Ash on the coffee table. In other words, Drew has become part of our household, and my boys are the better for it.[13]

What I've learned from this is that whether it's a friend or a neighbor or a widow or a foster child or someone else, people don't join our households just because you wish for them to. They become part of the household because there is a rhythm or a pattern that invites them in.

My friends who live a couple of blocks away, Derek and Sue, do this well. They don't have family in Richmond like we do,

---

13. One of the wonderful insights in Evert's book *The Spiritually Vibrant Home* and the Barna research behind it is that a significant factor in raising children who stick with the faith is having a meaningful relationship with a non-kin adult who follows Jesus.

so every Tuesday night they host a spaghetti dinner. It's simple and sustainable, and everyone on the block and more is invited. Just like our standing dinner with Drew, the rhythm pulls the outsider in.

So it is that family dinners are not just about the spiritual formation of those under our roof, they are about forming the household in the right direction and trying to draw the world in.

The Pepper Game, Again

Months after that fall vacation that almost went wrong, we were having our friends Barrett and Liza over for dinner. We had just sat down to eat when Whit jumped up and ran to the kitchen counter. Before I could scold him for leaving the table unannounced, he returned with the pepper grinder and handed it to our guests. "So here's what we're going to do," he started explaining. Suddenly my six-year-old was guiding a dinner party in the art of conversation. I couldn't have been prouder.

Like most habits of the household, I don't cling to family dinner because it's easy every night or because it makes the family work, I cling to it because I believe the rhythm is a keystone habit that is teaching something that I couldn't teach through words alone.

My prayer is that my kids grow up not just to intellectually know that the table is the center of gravity for relationships but to feel it because they've indwelt the rhythm for so long. My prayer is that decades from now we all still eat together and that many more than us are at the table, family and friends.

HABITS OF MEALTIMES
FORMING FAMILIES

Main Idea

Coming to the table is the keystone habit of forming relationships. When we make the table the center of gravity, it not only helps order the household, it pulls others in, turning strangers into friends.

Light a Candle

Candles help mark moments, especially for children. Keep a special candle and matches at the table for an opening ritual. Let kids participate, even if that's messy. Upon lighting, everyone says, "Christ is light."

Conversation Habits for the Table

Children, like us, learn to speak and listen in habits they observe. Try any of the below as norms for teaching the practice of conversation.

Things to try:

- Devices, for parents or kids, are not allowed at dinner, not even in pockets or on the table. They are silenced and somewhere else.
- Pass the pepper, or some other object, and have everyone answer the same question. After going once around the table, have the next person ask a new question.
- For bigger families with older children, try the "One Conversation Rule"—which means that you can talk about anything, but everyone has to be talking about the same thing instead of having multiple side conversations.

- Try a routine of everyone answering the same set of questions: for example, sharing one good thing and one bad thing. Perhaps add one funny thing for humor. If it's breakfast, have everyone share one thing they are excited about for the day.
- As parents, try telling simple stories about your day. The art of learning to take life and put it into stories is something children can learn at the table.
- Ask specific questions. Instead of general questions like "How was school?" that can be answered with one word, ask, "Who did you play with today?" or "What is one thing you did well today?" or "What is something that made you mad today?"

"The difference between people who happen to live together and families who befriend each other are rhythms of conversation at mealtimes."

Hospitality and Opening the Table

The household is expanded through inviting people to the table.

Things to try:

- If you can, have a table that is always big enough for an extra chair.
- Remember that standing invitations (like a guest every Tuesday) go much farther for hospitality than inviting someone over once in a while.
- Ideally, let guests bring something and help clean if they want. Inviting people into the prep and the mess means we are inviting them into the household, not just entertaining them.

- If you have extended family in town, consider setting up a weekly or monthly family dinner. If you don't, try asking some close friends to share a rhythm of eating with each other.
- Keep your food simple. The goal is not to impress but befriend.

Remember, you don't have to try everything at once. One small change can have big spiritual impact. Pick one thing to start.

Further Resources

The Spiritually Vibrant Home: The Power of Messy Prayers, Loud Tables, and Open Doors, Don Everts
The Gospel Comes with a House Key: Practicing Radically Ordinary Hospitality in Our Post-Christian World, Rosaria Butterfield

A Note on Adapting

Your meal may not be dinner, but it should be something. And maybe not every day, but more days than not so it feels like the norm.

We Always Need the Reminder of Grace: God's love inspires our action, but our action does not inspire God's love. Our family habits will not change God's love for us, but God's love for us should change our family habits.

CHAPTER 3

___

DISCIPLINE

I arrive home at 6 p.m. on a Tuesday. To my delight, at the sound of the knob turning, children begin yelling and scrambling to the door. On this particular day, Shep is the first to appear, bouncing around the corner wearing nothing but a diaper (my first clue to how the evening is going). He is sputtering, "Papa! Papa! Papa!" But all at once Coulter and Ash come careening around the corner at impressive speeds to overtake Shep's lead and get there first.

This is one of my favorite parts of the day. Everyone wants to be wanted, and I am no exception. But neither are any of the boys, and what was supposed to be a moment of reunion for all of us rapidly begins to turn into a battle. Shep is miffed that he didn't get to me first, but while he tries to squeeze in for a hug, I'm distracted by Coulter's brandishing a book to show me and Whit's coming down the stairs and yelling something about a bike ride. Amid this rising cloud of noise I grab up Shep and smile at him, trying to show him that he has my attention.

That's when he hauls off and smacks me in the face.

Lauren, who had just appeared on her way to greet me, stops and covers her mouth, clearly trying to hide her laughter.

I would not call myself a pushover. In my natural, unredeemed state, I'm prone to barking orders, sending people out of the room for small mistakes, and disciplining without counting to three. But Shep was a mere eighteen months old at the time of this particular smack. Surely, I think to myself, he didn't mean it. He is simply excitable. It was only a mistake.

So I hold a finger up to Coulter and Ash to wait, and I look at Shep and talk to him in my stern voice. "Sheppard!" (I now say his name like it's two words.) "Do not hit."

He looks at me, and I see the fullness of humanity staring back. I see the excitement, and the confusion. I see the churning development of the brain. I see the angels and the demons of his nature. I see war and peace and love and rage. I see myself. I see us all. I see a real live human being.

What I do not see is his left hand, as he hauls off and smacks me again. This time harder.

As we say, he has done it now. But the question is, what am I going to do?

I know exactly what I *want* to do in these moments. Whether it is Whit groaning when I ask him to help buckle his brother into the car seat, or Coulter saying "No!" when I tell him he needs to eat a bite of his broccoli, my instinct is usually clear: I want to find a way to control the situation.

What I don't want to do is the *real work of parenting*. I don't want to stop everything and do the work of understanding the fullness of my child's humanity, act and speak in an age-relevant way to engage his heart and mind, and try to balance the delicate mix of firm authority and gentle compassion that it takes to disciple this child toward love and reconciliation.

I would much rather manage this behavior in a way that's convenient for me, and I have a lot of tools that work pretty quickly for that: anger, physical force, sugar bribes, volume, false threats involving counting to three, cold shoulders, and more. But all of these are mostly designed for me to regain control of the moment.

Hence the problem: *moments of discipline are so hard because there is such a wide gap between what I want and what they need.*

What I want is control. What they need is loving, engaged discipline. And discipline is not a tool for controlling behavior. It is a process of discipling a child's heart toward the right loves. A tall order for a Tuesday evening at 6:02 p.m., when my face still stings. But this is the radical job of a parent, to take the ordinary moments of discipline and stitch them into a life of discipleship.

Discipline as Discipleship in the Story of God

The story of God and his people is one long story of raucous misbehavior.

If you ever get embarrassed about the problems in your family, just read the Bible. If you need more, take a skim through church history. We can tend to forget that the Old Testament is far too violent and sexual for TV, that Paul's letters dealt with many behaviors that were absolutely scandalous, and that the church throughout history has been just as marked by its moral failure as it has by its good deeds. When we say that "God so loved the world,"[1] it helps to remember that we are talking about the real world—the world of misbehaving people like you, me, and our kids.

And yet we also know from the story of the Bible that the dominant theme is not our misbehavior but God's love in spite of our misbehavior. Yes, we are fallen, broken, and depraved,

---

1. John 3:16.

but that's only one piece of the plotline. The far more important piece is that God loves fallen, broken, and depraved people. So much so that he sacrificed everything to love them out of their brokenness and into his fullness. "For God so loved [this depraved] world that he gave his one and only Son."

God's response to our misbehavior is to love us back into relationship, no matter the personal cost to him. Picture it like this: the biblical movement of discipline begins in love (creation), moves through human misbehavior (fall), continues through God's sacrifice in response to that misbehavior (redemption), and then calls us to action and ends in love and reconciliation again (consumation).

The plotline of the story of God is entirely shaped by the discipline of God, and that is a good thing, because that means it takes the shape of his love. Hebrews sums it up perfectly: "the Lord disciplines the one he loves."[2]

And this loving discipline of the heavenly father is what creates disciples who in turn love others like he loved us.[3] You do not need a degree in linguistics to see the root connection between discipline and discipleship. God's discipline is the process that creates God's *disciples*.[4]

This is profoundly relevant to the task of the parent. We shouldn't be surprised that the stories of our homes are constantly shaped by moments of discipline. If we love our children, then we will find ourselves faced over and over with the task of *discipling* our children through discipline, not as a means of controlling their behavior for our convenience but rather as a

---

2. Heb. 12:6.
3. John 13:34.
4. The words are so etymologically connected that sometimes it can be hard to tell them apart in a sentence. For that reason, and because I want to emphasize the importance of recasting moments of discipline as moments of *discipleship*, I will italicize *discipleship* throughout the rest of this chapter.

means of stewarding their hearts toward loving God. This is why discipline is both the highest call and the hardest thing we do as parents.

The Problem with Instincts

If discipline were easy, we wouldn't need to talk about practicing habits to guide us. We would just spontaneously respond with the right reaction. When a small child is about to run out into a street, for example, our instinct is the same every time, and it is always right—grab them. Protect them. It is simple, and it is never wrong. But discipline is not the same—not at all.

We need habits that help us practice discipline as *discipleship* because, frankly, we have all the wrong instincts. Discipline never happens at a moment of convenience. We are always too tired, or running late, or pulled in different directions, or something else. Even worse, depending on your upbringing and the harm that may have been done to you under the guise of discipline, you may carry an awful lot of awful baggage into these moments.

The first step in moving toward habits of discipline that help us *disciple* our children in these moments is trying to understand some of these problematic instincts we all go to.

INSTINCTS IN MOMENTS OF DISCIPLINE	
What We Think	"They are doing this on purpose."
Our Reaction	Anger directed at them
Our Mistake	This is an overdeveloped view of their fallenness. Our children are sinful fools in the most Proverbial sense of the term, yes, but they are also image-bearers in need of *discipleship*. In our exhaustion, we may think that their repeated disobedience is a personal assault intended to keep us from ever being happy. Fight against that lie.

What We Think	"This is an insult to me personally."
Our Reaction	Bitterness and revenge

	Our own selfishness can cause us to interpret childish behavior as a targeted attack—it is another version of thinking the world is all about us. At worst, this can lead toward blaming, shaming, and revenge. But it is so important in moments of discipline not to focus on our offense or inconvenience but on the opportunity of *discipleship* for them.
Our Mistake	

What We Think	"There's nothing wrong; they meant the best."
Our Reaction	Dismiss and ignore

	This is an overdeveloped view of innocence and an underdeveloped view of their fallenness. It is how we may be tempted to react, for example, when our child hurts someone else's child. We want to protect ourselves from the embarrassment of the reality that they harmed someone, so we dismiss it as just a mistake, even though our children unfortunately do intentionally hurt others, and that needs to be addressed and *discipled*, not ignored and dismissed.
Our Mistake	

What We Think	"They just misunderstood; they can be reasoned with. The problem is education."
Our Reaction	Useless words

	With young children in particular, this is an underdeveloped view of fallenness and also a major misunderstanding of child development. Their upstairs brain that deals with logic and rationality *is not ready for a speech, especially in a crisis moment.*[5] This means that we can waste opportunities for *discipling* young children by talking when we should be using body language and tone to help them *feel* the truth of what they cannot understand in words.[6] This certainly changes as kids get older, but not as much as we may think. Connecting with an older child emotionally, before you connect with them logically, is often the route that healing and reconciliation require. If we skip that and go straight to a speech, we're usually just talking to hear ourselves talk.
Our Mistake	

5. For some fantastic resources on understanding the psychology and neurology of children in both healthy and broken families, see Daniel J. Siegel and Tina Payne Bryson, *The Whole-Brain Child: Twelve Revolutionary Strategies to Nurture Your Child's Developing Mind* (New York: Bantam, 2012); Bessel van der Kolk, *The Body Keeps the Score: Brain, Mind, and Body in the Healing of Trauma* (New York: Penguin Books, 2015); and Adam Young's podcast, *The Place We Find Ourselves.*

What We Think	"I want them to feel pain and shame for what they've done. Then they'll learn."
Our Reaction	Revenge or abuse

Our Mistake	Whether in the form of a physical retaliation or verbal retaliation, when we lash out at children to make them hurt for what they did, *we are acting like children right at the moment when what they need is a parent*. Remember that the biblical concept of discipline begins and ends with God's love, *not with his anger*. Physical and emotional consequences may have a useful place as tools of discipline, but they are never to be vents for our own anger. When they do come, they need to come *after* we have done the work to manage our own anger and frustration.

What We Think	"I am frustrated and exhausted; I need to assert control to get the right result as fast as possible."
Our Reaction	Impatient behavior management

Our Mistake	This is an underdeveloped view of discipline. Discipline is not so we can get convenient behavior and have an easier life. It is to *disciple* the hearts of our children toward right loves. When discipline is just a way to gain control of the moment, we sacrifice momentary control for the real heart of parenting—the succession of *discipleship* moments, which over time form hearts in the love of God.

What We Think	"I could do this right if it weren't at this moment. This moment is really inconvenient."
Our Reaction	Abdication of the role of parent

Our Mistake	There is never an easy moment to discipline. That is not because of circumstance, it is because discipline is not easy. Ever. It is crucial to understand that our child's discipline is also about our own discipline. Part of our formation in parenting is learning that *we don't get a choice on when to drop everything and attend to our kids*. When we punt on discipline simply because it's inconvenient, we punt on the calling to be a parent.

---

6.   For example, in my moment, to give Shep a lecture about how hitting hurts would be pointless. Unfortunately, he knows that, and that's exactly why he did it. We, like our children, often hurt people because we feel emotionally hurt. My response to him needs to be far more rooted in engaging emotion and intangibles, because that's what caused the problem in the first place. We will get to how to do this in a few pages.

What We Think	"I am embarrassed and I need to manage my reputation here."
Our Reaction	Self-conscious behavior management
Our Mistake	Discipline is not about managing our children's behavior as a means to manage our own identity. But this is often our temptation, especially in public, and it is another inversion of discipline—we make it about us instead of them. Whether at the grocery store or a backyard gathering, we need to make sure the way we are responding to our children is not out of a fear of managing our identity in the moment but is about doing what our children need in that moment.

The list could go on. The ways we misunderstand discipline in moments of misbehavior are as infinite as our own misbehaviors. But note that all of the above mistaken instincts have something in common: when we see our children as problems to manage instead of image-bearers to be *discipled*, we end up making moments of discipline about our convenience instead of their *discipleship*.

This is as broken and selfish as it is natural and understandable. But it means that working on these problematic and dangerous instincts takes real practice, and that's where habits come in.

Habits can help interrupt the instincts that make discipline about us and our convenience, and train us to instead locate these moments in the story of God's *discipleship*—of us and our children.

The Pyramid of Discipline

If we want discipline in our homes to take the shape of *discipleship* in the story of God, we should consider how our habits in that moment can mirror the storyline of God's love for us and build toward reconciliation. The Pyramid of Discipline (fig. 2) is meant to be a resource to help you think about that movement.

It is not meant to be an exhaustive resource of discipline tactics or a checklist of things you need to do each time you discipline. It is rather a tool to help you visualize the kinds of habits you need to practice in order to move you, and your child, from misbehavior to reconciliation.

Figure 2. The Pyramid of Discipline

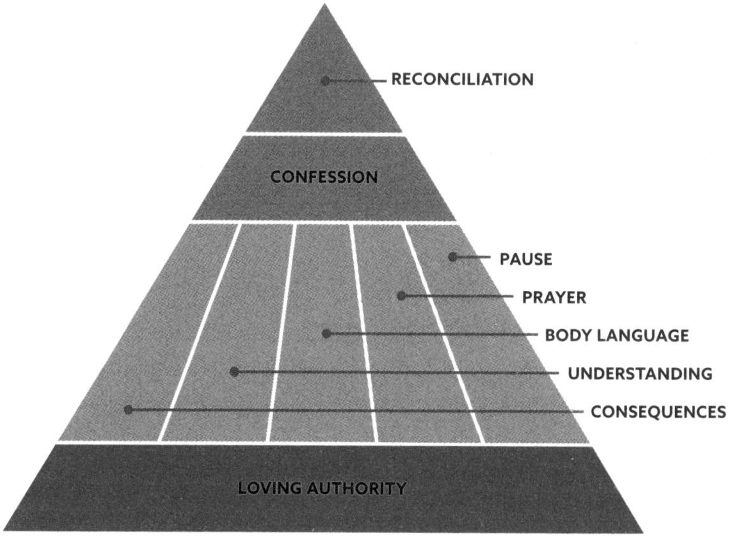

Habit 1: Establish Loving Authority

Loving authority is the foundation of discipline as *discipleship.* Some form of it will always be present. This might be picking a child up or intervening with a strong presence of tone or body language. It might mean sending someone home or demanding that you and a child take a walk together alone to talk. But whatever it is, it is involved and even interruptive. Authority intervenes with loving strength. It is the opposite of sitting on the sideline and making a request. We are not politely petitioning our children to consider our point of view, we are parenting them. This means we have a relational role to stand in, not just thoughts to offer. For their sake, we need to embrace the reality that we are in charge and that that is exactly what they need.

This is so important for protecting them from the consequences of their own self-destruction. Good parental authority protects them and the world from themselves. But even more, being authoritative in discipline is also about reinforcing a theological reality: a child is not autonomous. No one is. No one should be. The greatest harm any of us can do to ourselves and others is to seek a world without limits or authority.

So whether your kid is four or fourteen, they need a parent who is in charge and is going to wield authority in love as a knee-jerk reaction when something goes wrong.

Habit 2: Pause for a Moment

We are in charge, but we are far from perfect. Making some kind of pause a habit before discipline can allow us a chance to move from our instinctual reactions of anger or frustration to love and *discipleship*.

By nature, discipline happens in the moments when we are not prepared for it. When you planned the shopping outing on the way to the park, you did not plan for the twenty-minute meltdown in the aisle or the fight over bringing a snack onto the playground. This is the reality of discipline. It happens on the move, but it does not have to be off the cuff. Habits of pausing help with that.

This might be a timeout for your child or it may be a timeout for you to take a minute.[7] It may be a pause at the door before you

---

7. Timeouts are a great way to pause, but consider that a timeout is not the end goal of discipline. It is a pause to pass through so everyone can come back to their senses and handle this situation right. When everyone's fight or flight reflexes are engaged, a timeout or some other pause is a physiologically effective way for both of you to calm down and let the higher order brain take control.

open it to address the yelling going on inside or just a deep breath before you talk about what someone just said to you.

I will often tell my boys, "Wait here for a moment and then we will talk about this." The point is often not so that they can calm down but so that I can. They are image-bearers of God and deserve a parent who is going to approach them in love, not the explosive anger and frustration that I am so naturally prone to.

Habit 3: Pray and Talk to Yourself

I believe one of the key realizations of a maturing parent is when we finally see that moments of discipline are about us as much as they are about our kids. Yes, God is *discipling* our children in these moments, but if we're honest, most of it might be about how he is *discipling* us in those same moments. Parents need parenting.

For me, embracing this reality has been so helpful to changing the way I react to the moment. In these moments, we are dealing not just with our kids' selfishness over not sharing a video game controller but with our selfishness over not wanting to be interrupted to deal with this for the third time in five minutes. And only I can do the work to realize that my anger in that moment is not a product of their misbehavior but my impatience.

Our hearts need to be led to good places if we are going to lead the hearts of our children to good places. This is the kind of work that only prayer can do because words—especially the words of prayer and Scripture—lead the heart. So prayer and self-talk need to be habits that happen in that moment that we approach the situation.

For example, on the way to a moment of discipline (or during that pause I might be taking), I often pray to myself, "Lord, I am also [insert heart condition of child in trouble]. Help me to see that we both need to be parented by you." If possible, I might even mumble or whisper this out loud as I head upstairs to the site of the fight I'm about to break up. For example, if a child has hit his brother, it is very helpful to remind myself that I am also an angry person who wants to control the world through force. If they have disobeyed, I use a prayer to remind myself that I am also a proud person who dislikes authority. If they are scared, I use a prayer to remind myself that I am an anxious and panicky person too. Don't get me wrong, often I'm not nearly so clearheaded, and the prayer is just a silent inner scream for help. But often those are the most sincere prayers. And with time and practice, habits of prayer really can be developed, even in the most stressful of situations.

Do not underestimate the power of this short but real moment of prayer. The Lord has often used these moments to confront me with my own sin just as I am about to confront my child over theirs. And it is in that moment that I remember that I count on and long for the Lord's firm and gentle spirit. I too want someone who will save me from myself, but I also want someone who will comfort me. When I remember that in prayer, I become more willing to offer that spirit of both grace and truth to my kid. But if I do not pray as a habit of discipline, then I am by default making a habit of parenting alone in those moments, and that is dangerous for all of us.

Habit 4: Use Body Language and Space More Than Words and Threats

Have you ever considered all the intangibles that happen before we even open our mouths? I sometimes wonder in those moments whether I look like a raging maniac who is about to hurt them. Or whether I am giving them a stare that says, "I am disgusted with you." I often tell my sons not to complain with their shoulders, but they are not the only ones who need to be reminded of the body language lesson.

What your eyes and shoulders and hands are doing during these moments is communicating the love of the gospel—or something else—at least as much as your words are. When you can set a child in your lap to talk, or sit down on a bed beside a teenager, or kneel down to the eye level of a six-year-old, you should. When we can put a hand on their shoulder or look at them with love and not a scowl, we should. Remember, in the end, love is far more powerful than anger.

I repeatedly ask my boys to look in my eyes in these moments, not because I want to intimidate them but because getting the attention of their eyes and bodies is getting the attention of their minds and souls.

Space is equally as important. I think that's a part of why Jesus counsels us to pull a brother or sister aside and first confront them just between the two of you.[8] This kind of intimate and private space changes the way we talk and react to each other. There is a gracious wisdom in not embarrassing yourself or your child in front of everyone. It's almost common sense. When we pull aside, we get away from the pressure of other people watching. The reason disciplining your kids in front of your friends, your in-laws, or strangers at the grocery store is so hard is because you are watching them watch you and you have all the ghosts of their expectations hanging there. Your child is aware of this too. At home, when they call you a butthead, you might respond with an authoritative "No. We do not talk like that." At the playground, they do the same, and you say, "Sweetie, are we supposed to say that?" They smell blood in the water. You've shown your cards of inconsistency. No wonder they double-down and

---

8. Matt. 18:15–17.

call you a "double butthead." It's better that you and they both get a moment aside where your body and the space can help the communication instead of confuse it.

So remember that you are a full, embodied parent and that all of that comes to bear in moments of discipline as *discipleship*.

Habit 5: Be Relentless in Seeking Understanding

All the best and worst of us comes from the heart.[9] Ultimately, what we hope to do as parents is help our children understand their own hearts so they can experience heart repentance and change. Discipline without love is punishment for an act, but discipline as *discipleship* is training a child to become self-reflective. A parent's role is to try to really understand a child's heart in these moments because watching you do that is a way for them to learn how to understand their own hearts.

This means asking questions that lead them from knowing "what they did" to understanding why they did it. Questions that I rely on are not complicated, they simply explore what they felt and wanted as things happened. I usually use three "whats": (1) What did you do? (2) What did you think was going to happen when you did that? (3) What did you want the other person to feel when you did that?

Note that as we ask these questions, we're not searching for an excuse or even really an explanation, we're searching for them. When you ask a question—What did you think was going to happen when you threw that? Or what did you want her to feel when you stole that toy?—you are not asking it because you are going to reveal a good answer. There are no good explanations, there are only broken hearts. The right answer is usually, "Because I wanted to hurt him," or "I wanted to make her cry."

---

9. Prov. 4:23: "Above all else, guard your heart, for everything you do flows from it."

But that's not something to avoid or paper over. That is exactly what we need to hear, because that is a heart answer to *disciple*. "Son, it sounds like you are an angry person—a lot like I am. But God loves us anyway. And he can help us. You don't have to hit."[10] The conversation can go a lot of places from there.

It's hard to move them close to God and others when you don't know who they really are. Our efforts to understand them through questions or conversation show that we are not just out to control their behavior but out to find them, just as our heavenly father came to find us.

Habit 6: Think Carefully about Consequences

It is crucial that we learn that our sin has negative effects on ourselves and others. Actions have consequences. Some are even permanent. This is why giving consequences as a parent is an important responsibility. But it is also vital to remind yourself why you are here in the first place—we are trying to get to confession and reconciliation, not retribution. Consequences are helpful only insofar as they move us one step closer to reconciliation. Grounding a teenager or putting a kid in timeout may be helpful for stopping a dangerous or rude behavior, but that is not so much a consequence as a habit of pause—an intervention. The real work of reconciliation hasn't been done at all. So we should not see the consequence we provide as the end but rather as a means to the end.

In that sense, often, the consequences are inherent to the discipline process—not something we necessarily need to do after. It is a consequence that the playing had to stop. It is a consequence

---

10. We get better with this habit with our kids as we practice it on ourselves. I should ask myself, "What did I want to happen the other night when I slammed the cabinet so hard that I broke it?" The answer? "I wanted to break something because my anger is uncontrollable." Does that reveal a good reason? No. Does it reveal an important truth? Yes! I can be an angry person and I'm in need of repentance and grace. A parent who knows that about themselves parents better in a moment of discipline.

that we all had to repent. It is a consequence that we had to take the time and be vulnerable and discuss this. We are all raw and forgiven and reinstated—those are the most important consequences.

I—after much trial and error—am now weary of consequences that are unrelated to the process of reconciliation. First of all, I have never had much success with them. Taking away their dessert tomorrow night because they are whining at bedtime tonight is usually a pretense to get their attention. It is a threat I didn't really need. Further, it is also often a lie. We parents have terrible habits of forming our kids in confusion by telling them something that is going to happen when we count to three—and then not following through. (It's different if they are fighting over a toy and the consequence is taking the toy away. That is related, immediately understandable and helpful. But threatening "I'm not buying you any more toys" is both a lie and wasted words.)

As a result, I try to be really wary of consequences that are unrelated to the moment or to reconciliation. Instead, I look for consequences that give us the time and the space to be reconciled. For example, one of my go-to consequences if a child is disobedient or disrespectful is that they work a chore alongside me. Instead of forcing them away where we both stew in our anger, we are forced into the same space, into cooperation, and into words that start to soften us.

The best consequences are the things that push us back toward loving God and each other, because that's where discipline as *discipleship* is trying to go. Usually, that will involve confession and repentance.

Habit 7: Insist on Apologies as Confession

If repentance is the actual turning of our hearts from sin, think of confession as the step where we have to say our sin out loud so we realize how nasty it is, which helps make us want to turn from it. We help our children learn to repent when we make a habit of helping to lead them to confession.

It may be helpful to remember that no one wants to do this, so expect a hard-hearted and begrudging participant. That is okay—what we are doing here is looking for liturgies to help soften our hearts.

Consider how this plays a role in worship services. We say words of confession not always because we mean them (yet) but because we want to mean them.[11] Think of apologizing or confessing as ways of saying the things we desperately don't want to say so we can mean the things we desperately want to mean. Words lead the heart, and we have to lead the hearts of our children by leading them through words they may not want to say.

For our family, whether it is Lauren or me or the boys, when someone confesses or apologizes, we have to look someone in the eye and say exactly what they did out loud. Mumbling is not enough. "Okay, fine! Sorry!" is not enough. Looking at the ground and saying something is not enough, either. This is not because I'm trying to be a tyrant, it is because liturgy matters.

When we look at someone and say the words we should mean as if we do mean them, something happens. *We start to mean it.* The words and the process change us because we are acting in cooperation with grace in that moment.

Note that this might very often be us. The place Lauren and I have to apologize to our kids the most is in the process of discipline, where we went too far. Don't miss the opportunity to repent in front of them if you have wronged them.

Embracing the habit of working toward confession and

---

11. We actually do, deep down there somewhere, want to repent. Because turning and repenting means being free of the chains that enslave us. It's throwing off all the heavy weights so our hearts drowning in the sea of our own sin can finally bob back to the surface of grace. Repentance is exactly what we want. But we need words to lead us there.

apology is not a magic incantation that works the same way every time, but it is a wise obedience that opens our hearts to repentance and grace.

Habit 8: Always End in Reconciliation

No matter where we might begin, we are always building to reconciliation. There are all kinds of ways to do this, but we must insist on doing something.

In our house, we have a small liturgy of reconciliation called the "Brothers' Hug." For example, when two of them break out into one of their hourly fights, we separate them (habit of pause), talk to them (habit of understanding), and have them apologize (habits of confession), and maybe there is a consequence too. This is all very important, but this process is not over until they do a Brothers' Hug. This means a hug that lasts until both (not just one of them) cracks a smile or laughs. For the littles, this is usually a giggle, because a Brothers' Hug usually turns into a new wrestling match. For the older ones it might take tickling or a joke or some tears, but until they can look at each other and smile, we are not there yet.

Is a forced smile okay? Absolutely. It's by acting like we're sorry and reconciled that we cultivate the desire to repent and be reconciled. And the act of holding someone and smiling is where they remember that life is much more fun when we play rather than fight. A Brothers' Hug is a small act of practice for the way the world should be.

Even as their parent, I use this practice of a reconciling hug too. If you recall the bedtime liturgy, it is hard for me to be a tyrant during bedtime when I know that that moment of blessing and prayer is coming. The habit of knowing where I'm going changes how I get there. Likewise, knowing a reconciling hug is coming changes the movement of discipline. This is perhaps the summary of this chapter: we parent differently when we know that discipline is *discipleship* that must end in love and laughter.

It's hard to berate your child when you know that you both are going to have to hug and smile when this is over. If I get to the end of a discipline moment and I am still so mad that I cannot hug or tickle or joke with them, then I probably have not done it right. If I can't make a joke or get my kid to laugh at the end of a cycle of discipline, then I know I've probably been too harsh. If I don't even want to, I know I've probably disciplined out of anger and not love.

So the liturgy of reconciliation provides an anchor weight that helps make sure I end in the right place.

The Pyramid in Practice

With all this in mind, we come back to me, standing in the doorway after having been smacked by a toddler. He is in need of authority, and I am in need of a pause. So I give him a stern no, but also a secret wink to the rest of the family—to remind him that I'm in charge, but to remind all those watching that you don't have to be angry to be in charge; usually anger is not a sign of authority but a sign of those who fear they are losing authority.

Then I take Shep upstairs. I wanted to greet the whole family, but *discipleship* does not happen at our convenience. Further, the walk up the stairs gives me a moment to pause and pray, "Lord, help me remember that when I feel lonely and ignored I too lash out at those I love." I put Shep on my lap and look in his eyes so he knows that I'm in charge but he also knows that the person who is in charge is the same person who loves him.

While he's on my lap, I remind him, "We don't hit. Can you say, 'Yes, Papa'?" He turns away in defiance. I say it again. And then again, because we're not going to leave this moment until he says it. At this point in his development, he can't apologize. But he can repeat words that I say, and that is a signal of obedience. The words lead his heart too, and when he finally relents and says, "Yes, Papa," you can see his whole demeanor change. He has come under authority, and he is noticeably happier for it. This is his way of confessing. Before he has his own words to confess, he gets parented to the essence of confession by saying words he's supposed to say.

And now, the most important part: I tickle him. And I hug him. We're pals again, because that's what reconciliation means. We can walk back downstairs laughing together, and that's the point.

It's not easy, of course, and it has to be done over and over and over. But rather than complaining about it, we'd do better to remember that to get it to sink in, the biblical movement toward reconciliation has to be practiced. Which means we're simply acting out the drama of redemption again and again, but this is a story that never gets old.

Discipline as Acting the Drama of Redemption

One Thursday night, a couple of minutes after putting the boys to bed, I heard shuffling. When I went back in, I found that Coulter and Ash had been busy ferrying all of Coulter's bedding across the room to Ash's bottom bunk. This consisted of a remarkable nest of cozy things, including your standard sheet and blanket, an enormous teddy bear twice Coulter's size, seven smaller stuffed creatures, five or six little muslin blankies he likes to roll into a ball and hug, two pacifiers (both of which he was too old for), and a water bottle and pillow.

Needless to say it was a significant haul. And honestly, when I opened the door, I was kind of proud. They had done it all in the dark and the whole point was so that they could have a slumber party in Ash's bed. So I tipped my hat and said, "Well done. Have fun." I told them as long as they were quiet that was fine and went back downstairs.

The problem was, an hour later, they were still kicking each other and cracking jokes, so I moodily moved everything back to Coulter's bed and told them no more noise. They finally went to bed.

However, the next night they asked if they could do it again. I said no. I made it *really* clear. "You all could not be quiet trying to sleep in the same bed last night, so no getting out of your beds tonight, okay? I want everyone to stay in their beds." Everyone gave their assent. There was a meeting of the minds. There was no ambiguity. A verbal contract was made.

So when I heard the footsteps a couple of minutes later, I tiptoed to the door, whipped it open, and flipped on the lights in the all-at-once approach. It worked.

I caught Ash midstride across the room, carrying a load of stuffed animals to Coulter's bed. He looked as guilty as I thought he would. And as scared too.

One of the things I love about brothers close in age is that they kind of root for each other when one is in trouble. I will often get a plea for mercy from the sidelines: "He didn't actually hit him that hard. I saw him, it was just *kinda* hard." As I sat down in the rocking chair in their room and asked Ash to stand in front of me, I noticed Coulter watching from his bed nervously.

"Ash, what were you doing?" I asked.

"Moving Coulter's stuff," he answered.

"And what did I say about that?" I asked.

"Not to do it," he answered.

"So were you disobeying on purpose?" He winced. I could tell from his pursed lips that he felt bad and was struggling to keep his composure.

"Yes." He looked down.

Remember, words lead the heart. There are reasons we do slow, precise confessions, because voicing reality reminds us of the weight of reality, and in this case as Ash admitted that he disobeyed on purpose, I could see the remorse and guilt fill his eyes. He knew he had messed up; he looked embarrassed and scared. Here was the consequence—he didn't need anything else. And here was the understanding—I didn't need anything else. In his trembling face I saw a picture of my own heart—that trembling thing, half embarrassed and half scared, full of the knowledge that I am not quite right and I always mess stuff up.

He wanted to cry right then and there because he felt broken, he definitely felt caught, he probably felt stupid, and he seemed to feel scared. So we talked for a minute. "Is that a bad thing to disobey?" I asked.

"Yes," he admitted. As he did, he began to cry.

"And what do you need to say to me if you disobey me?"

"Sorry." He sniffled.

"So can you look in my eyes and say sorry?" He blinked his tears away and did it, but he still looked more scared than sorry.

"And then what am I going to say to you?" I asked him.

He stopped crying. "That you forgive me?" That was the right answer, he knew it, but he looked almost surprised—like it couldn't be true again this time.

"That's right. Ash." I looked into his eyes, "I forgive you. And what do I say about how I feel about you when you do a bad thing?"

"That you love me anyway?"

"That's right. And what do we need to do now?"

"A hug until we smile," he said.

So we did. I squeezed him until he smiled, even though he still had tears in his eyes.

That is when I noticed little Coulter. Far off to the side in his little bed, he had started bouncing with an uncontrollable smile. When we hugged, he started cheering and pumping his fist in the air.

And why shouldn't he? Aren't we acting out the drama of salvation in our own small way? Aren't we rehearsing and practicing the narrative of forgiveness and reconciliation? We're not just telling it to each other, we're participating in it. Trying it out from all angles. Testing the story and seeing that it fits. Indeed, what we seem to want and need over and over is to remember and relive forgiveness. After all, reconciliation is the story of the world. If it's not the story of our families, then bitterness will be.

Discipline, when it becomes *discipleship*, is something worth practicing and crying over, laughing and hugging over, and something worth cheering for too.

HABITS OF DISCIPLINE
FORMING CHILDREN

Main Idea

Ordinary moments of discipline can build a life of discipleship. But discipline often becomes about our controlling our kids' behavior. Habits help interrupt bad instincts of control and anger and build new patterns of love and discipleship of the heart.

"This is the radical job of a parent, to take the ordinary moments of discipline and stitch them into a life of discipleship."

On Short Moments

Most of our discipline happens in moments, not drawn-out engagements. So think about how ending with a smile, tickle, laugh, or hug can briefly signal reconciliation and prevent us from creating a long line of ughs, sighs, or scowls throughout the day.

Remember, discipline is probably the hardest thing we do as parents. Give a lot of grace, to you and your kids.

Further Resources

No-Drama Discipline: The Whole-Brain Way to Calm the Chaos and Nurture Your Child's Developing Mind, Daniel J. Siegel and Tina Payne Bryson
Parenting: Fourteen Gospel Principles That Can Radically Change Your Family, Paul David Tripp

A Note on Adapting

Habits of discipline (rightly!) vary significantly, depending on age, family history, and child personality. But God's story of love and discipleship does not change. Wherever you are, use this as a time to rethink how your norms of discipline can be norms of love, reconciliation, and discipleship.

We Always Need the Reminder of Grace: God's love inspires our action, but our action does not inspire God's love. Our family habits will not change God's love for us, but God's love for us should change our family habits.

CHAPTER 4

SCREENTIME

I remember the night Lauren told me that things were going to change.

"You're going to what?!" I blurted out. "But their hour of screentime is the only break you get in the afternoon!"

"It's just not worth it," she said. She didn't look excited. She didn't look happy.

She just seemed resigned to fighting for something better than what we had. What we had was a screentime rut.

It didn't take long after having our first child to realize that the screen did something magical to children. Our first, Whit, absolutely hated the car—unless, of course, "Elmo's Song" was playing. I remember thinking that this seemed like some sort of magic drug.

From that point on, we were relatively moderate with our screentime, but it was still a regular staple in their daily routine. As the second and third kid came around, the struggle to find even a twenty-minute stretch in the afternoon where kids were either napping or resting seemed impossible—unless we gave them an iPad. In which case they would sit watching a couple of shows and give Lauren a "break" for an hour—a break just being an hour she could catch up on all the other work of the home.

It is hard to overemphasize how difficult the nonstop nature of parenting is. In the young years of parenting, you wake to children. You eat with children. You run errands with children. You play with children. Some of the most common desires of all people are denied you: just to have an adult conversation, focus on a task, or complete something—all of these are taken from you. I often think about how a typical parent's desire just to stand off to the side of the playground and scroll on a device makes so much sense—the mental difficulty of being surrounded by children all day is so intense, it makes anyone want to check out. For so many parents, screens are the only way out of this madness. That was true for Lauren's one hour each afternoon.

The problem was what happened afterward. The fallout seemed to be getting worse and worse. It was a fight to turn off the shows, and they seemed fidgety and short-tempered with each other afterward. They were even more needy and full of complaints.

This was the rut we were in when Lauren told me of her decision to remove screentime from their daily routine. But years later, she stands by the decision and still makes it every day. Recently I asked her why.

"Because the fight is worth it," she said. "The fight is not about 'Are screens okay?' or 'How much screentime is too much?' The fight is about whether you are forming your children or you are defaulting to letting screens form them. This is a fight for formation, and that is never easy, but it will always be worth a parent's time and energy—even if it's the last bit of time and energy you have."

Who Forms Who? The Fight for Formation Is Worth It

I like that Lauren phrased the fight over screens as a fight for formation, because that is the central reason screens are so important. In the story of God, we are all becoming someone—this is the biblical idea of formation.

My favorite summary sentence on this is from Romans 12:2: "Do not conform to the pattern of this world, but be transformed by the renewing of your mind." Paul seems to assume that formation is the default—we are either being formed (conformed) to the world or being formed (transformed) by God. This is an important lesson about what a human heart is—it is never *not* being shaped by something. The human heart is not a car: *there is no neutral.* So we must always pay attention to what is grabbing the attention of our minds and imaginations—because where the imagination goes, so goes the heart.[1]

Screens are incredibly formative because they convey stories and images that captivate our imaginations. This doesn't make them bad; it makes them powerful, and power can be for good or bad. But the fact is, for both us parents and our children, we will either form our screen habits or our screen habits will form us. There is no alternative. This is a fight over who forms who.

Consider the stakes for a moment. If we do not teach our kids about sex, screens will be happy to do it for us. If we do not teach them categories of good and evil, then screens will be happy to obscure all of them. If we do not teach them that God made them who they are on purpose, man or woman and black or white, then screens will be happy to confuse their understanding of all of these things. If we do not teach them that buying things will not make them happy and that consumption always leaves you hungrier, then screens will teach them that being a consumer is a way to status and satisfaction. If we do not teach them that the world of nature is ferocious and fantastic, something to be

---

1. For an in-depth and practical take on this connection between our imaginations and our loves, see James K. A. Smith's work *You Are What You Love: The Spiritual Power of Habit* (Grand Rapids, MI: Brazos, 2016).

stewarded and stunned by, then the world of screens will teach them that looking at pictures of nature is enough. If we do not teach them that silence is a sacred place where God speaks to us, then screens will make sure they never, ever discover it. If we do not teach them that vulnerable and embodied friendship is the heart of the good life, then screens will relentlessly nudge them toward "connecting" and "liking" their way to endemic loneliness.

If that is not enough, screens are functionally among the strongest habit-forming mechanisms we experience outside of addictive drugs. These electronic drugs are lying all over our house: they are on the desks and the walls, in our pockets and purses; they hang over our mantles and sit beside our beds. Free drugs everywhere—what do we think our kids will do if we don't parent them otherwise?

Screens are as powerful as they are ubiquitous, which means the default of modern life is going to be limitless screens unless a parent intervenes and teaches that limits are a good thing, especially when it comes to screens.

Limits as the Guardrails to the Good Life

At the core of being a parent is the idea of setting limits for your children. "Not that close to the street." "That's enough hot chocolate." "It's bedtime." "No more shows." "You can't sleep over if their parents aren't home." "It's time to let someone else have a turn." The list goes on ad infinitum. Sometimes, I reflect with sheer awe on the number of times I say no in a single day. While I strongly encourage figuring out how to redirect attention to something else ("We can't hit your brother with that bat, but we can hit this ball! Look, it's fun!") and affirm the pursuit of better things ("I know chocolate is good, but you don't want a tummy ache later, right?"), when it comes down to it, it's simply a key part of your job description to protect your child from their infinite desire.

Dwell on this with me for a moment, because this is the human condition. In this respect, we are all children: our core struggle is to want it all. This was the struggle in Eden—to want to be limitless like God, to eat the fruit and be like him. This is why Proverbs counsels us to put a knife to our throats before we desire the food at a king's table.[2] This is why Jesus counsels us to cut off our right hand if it causes us to sin.[3] The violence of the imagery is serving a purpose. Our ever-expanding desire for more options will cut us off unless we decide to cut it off. Our infinite desires will do violence to us and others unless we control them and put them in their proper place. This is a matter of healthy limits.

In the American story, limits are bad. They get in the way of our freedom, which means we need to get rid of all limits to be happy. But in the story of God, limits are the way to the good life, even the way to happiness. We know this because Jesus took on the limits of being a man, disciplining himself into a life of sacrifice—why? So that we could be free from the ultimate limitation of sin and death. "It is for freedom that Christ has set us free," Paul writes.[4] True, biblical freedom comes through finding the right limitations—not getting rid of all limitations.

In a classic image of freedom within constraints, G. K. Chesterton writes, "We might fancy some children playing on the flat grassy top of some tall island in the sea. So long as there was a wall round the cliff's edge they could fling themselves into every frantic game and make the place the noisiest of nurseries. But the walls were knocked down, leaving the naked peril of

---

2. Prov. 23:1–3.
3. Matt. 5:30.
4. Gal. 5:1.

the precipice. They did not fall over; but when their friends returned to them they were all huddled in terror in the centre of the island; and their song had ceased."[5]

Perhaps we can say, then, that the role of parents is to put up the fences that create the playground. It is by carefully choosing the right limits that the playground of the good life is found.

Taking the Pain so Your Children Don't Have To

Before this gets too rosy, let's note the practical pain of this in real life. Setting boundaries for your children is never fun. It is rarely easy, and it always requires a lot of wisdom.

On the pain of setting screentime limits, Lauren reminded me, "The cost is for us to bear. It's going to be hard—yes. One of the hardest things you do. They are going to want them—all the time. And even more, you are going to want them all the time, to make your afternoon or your car ride or your morning easier. There is a true loss to a parent's time and capacity. But as parents we take the pain now so our kids don't have to later."

As usual, Lauren is right. We can't talk about the practical habits of setting screentime limits without addressing how difficult that is. But before you resign and say, "This just won't work for me and our family," gently remind yourself of the sobering yet beautiful call of the parent: as Jesus took the pain so that we don't have to, so we take the pain so our children don't have to. The story of the gospel is not just our greatest hope in life and death, it is also the best paradigm for parenting. We don't sacrifice our kids' formation so that we can have an easier life. We sacrifice the ease of our life so our kids can have biblical formation.

In this way the battle over screentime takes the shape of God's

---

5. G. K. Chesterton, *Orthodoxy* (New York: John Lane Company, 1909).

redemptive love. We aid our children's formation in character, wisdom, emotional intelligence, and creativity by intervening as parents and taking the inconvenience of saying, "Yes, this is going to mean I get fewer breaks and have to be more involved and have to manage constant requests, but this is for their formation, which means it is a fight worth fighting well."

The Power of Curation

If the battle of screens is a battle for formation, then curation, not abstinence, is the answer. If screens were simply harmful or evil, then this would be a lot simpler—just stay away from them. But screens—like most technologies—are far more nuanced than that, which makes our task much more complicated, because it is almost always harder to use something responsibly than it is just to stay away entirely.

To do this well, we need a two-part concept of curation. Curation means first, that we are setting limits, and second, that we are choosing well within those limits.

The First Step of Curation: Setting Limits

The best way to think about practically setting limits for screens is setting expected rhythms. For example, I will watch a movie with the family on Friday night, and I will watch a Netflix series with Lauren on our Wednesday date night, but aside from that, I generally won't be watching movies or shows.

This means that on a regular Monday night, I don't have to use the mental energy to consider my options. After the kids' bedtime, I might do some work, clean the kitchen and listen to a podcast, read a book, or listen to the Nationals on the radio, but I know I won't be watching streaming media because it's not one of those nights.

For our children, this paradigm is similar. One of the hardest things we have done as a household is break them from the "screentime might be any time" mentality and steered them into expected rhythms of engagement. (Does this mean they don't ask? Of course not! They constantly ask. But does it mean they ask less and understand the answer will be consistent when it's given? Yes. And that is something.)

Here are some expected rhythms of engagement we have used to function within healthy limits.

Family Movie Nights

At our house, Friday night is family movie night. Often, we answer the question, "Can we watch a show?" with the question, "Is it Friday?" If not, they get the point. If so, they know that means, "Yes, after dinner tonight." But the upshot of this is we get to talk about (fight about?) what we'll watch together. We get to share the same experiences of watching the same movies and laughing about them or talking about them. Sometimes we all sit down and watch; often Lauren and I use it as an excuse to let all the boys watch something while we catch up on cleaning or just relax. Whether it is on a Friday or another day, a family movie night is not only a way to set an expected rhythm of watching something communally but also a way to say yes to some times and no to other times in a consistent way.

Screenless Car Rides

We have said no to screens in the car, as a matter of normal life. I have taken a lot from Andy Crouch's wisdom in *The Tech-Wise Family* that car time is conversation time.[6] I find this to

---

6. Andy Crouch, *The Tech-Wise Family: Everyday Steps for Putting Technology in Its Proper Place* (Grand Rapids, MI: Baker, 2017).

be so true. Especially when it's a one-on-one drive, traveling can be a wonderful time for talking. So in general, car time is not screentime. This means that the kids don't have to constantly wonder whether they can play with a phone or some other device every time they get in the car. They now know that is not the case. (Recall that we began otherwise, with "Elmo's Song" and YouTube being ways to ease every drive. While changing is hard, it's important to know it is not impossible. It is very possible, even when it takes work.) However, they also know the exceptions to this rule. For example, on special trips like the three-hour drive to visit Lauren's parents, "Yes!" They will get to watch a movie on the second half of the drive, after they have read something. And this is also a normal rhythm they anticipate and look forward to.

Sunday Cousin Movies
When the whole, extended Earley family gets together every Sunday to sabbath and lunch together, the kids all get to watch a movie downstairs. This is both to give them the fun of watching something with their cousins and (admittedly) so that the adults can more easily talk and eat together for a meaningful period of time. I think it's important to note here that parents tend to feel the natural guilt of using screens as a babysitter, especially if it is happening all the time. That is probably something to pay attention to. But when there are curated rhythms of expected engagement, it is wise stewardship of time as a parent to pick times where you can also enjoy the time. For us, cousin movies on Sunday are a way for them to all watch a chosen movie communally (which is, we should note, far different from streaming on auto-play alone with a device in a corner) and also a way to make the sabbath afternoons with our family special.

Movies at Friends' Houses

Part of curating well and setting good family limits means recognizing that everyone is fighting their own battle. It is hard enough to do this work without us parents constantly judging each other for our differing choices. So I strongly encourage you to be confident of your own choices, but gracious in judging other parents' choices. If someone had encountered us years ago, they might have thought, "Wow, they don't really have many limits." That is where we were in our journey. Every family has a journey, and every family has good and bad phases and different values. So within reason, I think it's wise and important to respect other people's rhythms. That means when the boys go over to a friend's house and are spontaneously invited to watch a movie, that is usually okay. But the flip side of this is that, yes, we monitor things like content and how they watch whether they are here or somewhere else.

For example, they know they are *never* allowed to just go somewhere and watch a screen without asking a parent. When they are young, they cannot even be on a screen without a parent in the room. And likewise, when kids come over to our house, it is a rule that they cannot be on a device—period—unless we monitor it. Neighborhood kids come over to play all the time, but if they happen to have an iPhone, they cannot sit on our couch and watch it alone. Our rule is that they are here to play with everyone, or they have to go home—and guess what? They always choose to play.

Rhythms of Screen Sabbaths

When we live into our rhythms above, we end up with a couple of days each week where screens are just not turned on for entertainment (as distinct from school or work). Depending on where your family is in this process, one wise baseline practice is simply to start somewhere by declaring one day a week a sabbath from screens.[7] This may be the first step toward establishing some expected rhythms of off times, and it may do well for you as a parent too, especially if you pick Saturday or Sunday where the family can focus on time together instead.

Generous Exceptions

Despite all this wisdom of rhythms as limits, one thing that is not uncommon at all is an exception on a bad day. If someone is sick, then it is very likely they will be watching movies all day. If a ballgame or a much-anticipated playdate gets rained out, then a consolation prize of watching an iPad and a show is not unusual. This is to say not only that exceptions prove the rules (normally these things are not happening) but also that it goes to show the point is not to obey the rule for the rule's sake but to let limits guide you into wise decision making. If someone has done something exceptional and deserves a reward, maybe a spontaneous movie night is in order. Or sometimes, it has just been an awful day and we say, "Let's abandon family dinner, get takeout, and let the kids watch something." This shouldn't be regarded as failure. It should be seen as the fruit of healthy rhythms. Creating wise patterns allows you the space to improvise and make wise and even generous exceptions.

Off Time as the Norm

Part of curating expected rhythms of screentime means emphasizing that the time outside of those rhythms is off time. Notice that if you add up all of the above, there's a good amount of screentime in our weekly rhythms. No one can call us Luddites. But when it is not those times, we are playing cards or board games, we are outside building something, or we are inside

---

7. Crouch, *The Tech-Wise Family.*

reading something. And in the aggregate, those times of physical, engaged, creative, and collaborative play *far* exceed the other times. And this is the goal.

Practical Tips to Starting New Curation Rhythms

As you consider setting limits by creating your own rhythms as the first step of curation, my first piece of practical advice is to make them serious and stick to them. It is always difficult to enforce new boundaries and create new expectations, but children pick up on habits quickly if we hold to them for a couple of days. So don't announce something unless you're going to follow through, but when you do announce something, stick to it.

Second, the right amount of screentime is almost certainly something less than you are comfortable with. This is also hard. But the reality is that being a parent is hard because setting limits is hard, and the best thing for our kids is probably choosing something that is less than we would like.

Finally, note the value of the nudge here. One of the other valuable pieces of wisdom from *The Tech-Wise Family* is the idea of creating space to push yourself in the right direction. For example, a while ago we spent a few hundred dollars restoring the fireplace in our family room. This money could have been spent on an amazing flat-screen TV to hang above the mantle, but we have decided that we want it to be easier to have a fire than to watch a movie in our family room. We do have a cool little projector, so when we watch Friday night family movies, we move the little paintings from above the fireplace, set them on the mantle, and then set up the projector on the coffee table. It's awesome for watching a movie because of the way the picture takes up the whole wall, but on the other hand, it's a pain to pull out and set up—and we want it to stay that way.

The nudge means it is just much easier to start a fire in our living room and pull a guitar off the wall or a board game from the shelf than it is to pull out the projector for a movie. At the end of the day, curating space helps us curate time and relationships too. It nudges us to make good choices—which is the very important second step of curation.

The Second Step of Curation: Choosing Well

While setting limits is crucial to making good choices with screentime, it is not, by itself, enough. There is a limit to the usefulness of limits. At the end of the day, we need to decide how to fill the space we have with good choices. Here are some ideas for that.

Choose Good Content over New Content

Often, the nudge of auto-play combined with a fear of missing out makes us unconsciously default to watching new content. But there is no reason to assume something is worth watching simply because it is new. In fact, we should probably lean toward the opposite assumption. It is much easier to choose well when something has stood the test of time.

Lauren and I have started forming our kids' movie canon, beginning with the great movies of Disney and Pixar we watched when we were young—many of which we still love watching. Likewise, we take them through the great stories that we grew up with, from Star Wars and The Lord of the Rings to Harry Potter and more.

In general, I take it as a warning sign if I can't stand watching what my kids are watching. Good stories are captivating, whether they are kid or adult movies, and one of the ways we filter out bad stories is by waiting to see if they last.

Pick Media That Expands or Educates

Pick media that expands the imagination or educates the mind, not media that simply stimulates. This sounds complicated in words, but it is simple in practice. You can be a fairly good judge of this after watching five minutes of any show with your kids. For example, I watch some shows with them and immediately intuit that this is basically educational content but produced to be interesting to kids—like *Sesame Street*, *Mister Rogers' Neighborhood*, or something new, like *Wild Kratts* (which teaches kids about animals). On the other hand, there are good story cartoons that take kids through a long narrative or a series of short narratives. These are both great.

But then there are shows—often cartoons—that rely on rapidly changing scenes and noises just to keep kids' attention. You don't have to be a brain scientist to see that there is no story; it just overloads the mind the same way a lab-designed potato chip captivates the tongue with excess salt. These are problematic not just because they are a waste of time but more because they train us to sit and submit to the twists and turns of media—rather than do the work of paying attention to a good story or following educational content. At the end of the day, *how* we watch is equally as important as *what* we watch, and one of the most important things we can teach our kids is to actually pay attention, not just tune out and stare.

Be Present

Spend less time thinking about whether "bad words" are present and more time thinking about whether you are present. If we spent half the time we spend worrying over "appropriateness" on watching with our kids and processing and engaging with the content they watched, we would take a big step in the right direction. The world is not safe. It's certainly not appropriate.

Think about what you read and see and hear on the TV and the internet without even trying to pay attention. An essential skill of growing up is knowing how to react to explicit language, violence, sex, or dangerous ideas. It's far more wholesome to know what to do with those things rather than imagine that we can somehow avoid them entirely.

Our goal is not to protect our children from the world of immorality *out there* but to teach them how to deal with the immorality that is out there *and in here too*. This means parents have to do the hard work of explaining the brokenness of the world and how we're just the same kinds of broken people, rather than trying to keep brokenness from becoming a conversation topic at all.

While I can speak only anecdotally, I have noticed in my own childhood a real difference between the kids who were raised with implausibly strict media boundaries and the ones who were, within boundaries, allowed to mature alongside their parents. The former tended to lose respect for their parents' impossible rules and consequently cast out all rules, while the latter tended to learn how to pick what to watch well.

One of my favorite childhood movies is *The Sandlot*. When I showed it to my kids for the first time, I was reminded that Wendy Peffercorn is very objectified by the film—every time she comes on the screen, there are slow shots panning her body and bathing suit, and so on. Even worse, the famous scene where Squints tricks Wendy into a nonconsensual kiss is, well, not okay at all. It's never something I would teach my boys to do. So it was a good opportunity to pause the movie and talk about it, which we did, right then and there. We talked about how you never ever touch a girl against her will or without her permission, period. We talked in simple terms about how every single boy is going to struggle with seeing the world through a sexualized lens. With four boys, this is a conversation I'm going to have over and over and over, and that night we were better for having had that conversation rather than pretending it doesn't exist. Moreover, there are themes of friendship and courage and the love of sport that far outweigh the mischievous way the kids got ahold of chewing tobacco.

Certainly, there are categories of sex, violence, or themes that are too mature, too much for a kid to process, or too likely to confuse their innocence (which is one of the precious gifts of childhood). But at some point, kids must wade into the world, and far better that we are there with them when they do. Watching content together, even inappropriate content, means that we get that opportunity in unique ways. I will not be there the first time someone in school says a demeaning joke about a girl's body to my sons. But I can be there in movies where they do—and I can prepare them for how to react. That's the value of engaging in media *with* our kids.

Make a Watch List

We shouldn't expect to help our kids make good watching choices if we don't spend any time on it. One of the ways Lauren and I think ahead in this area is that we keep a list of movies and shows the kids should watch. Lauren often reads movie reviews—they exist for kids' movies too!—and then puts them on a list. We do this for reading, and this is equally invaluable for watching.

This is also a way to develop a "canon," so to speak—the things that are worth watching over and over. I think this is a virtue that is overlooked in the streaming age. When you rewatch good movies or shows, you pick up on new things, you memorize lines, you let the good themes sink in deep. You feel the world of the story in a deeper way.

Note that something really fundamental is happening when we take the time to do this. When we make a list of great content and walk our kids through it, we are taking the power of cura-tion back from the algorithms of companies. Consider this: no matter what your flaws, you are a way better parent than Google is. You can make better choices for your children than streaming media companies do—because you make them for the sake of love, not profit. But when we do nothing rather than something, we default to letting technology companies curate media for our children. We let them parent our children. So remember, someone will curate what they watch, it might as well be you.

Watch Communally, Then Process Communally

For adults and for kids, we all make better choices when we are not alone. Movies and shows have a unique capacity to bind us together and give us shared language, but this happens only when we watch together, laugh together, ask questions together, and process afterward.

There is a rule in our house that you have to watch the cred-its (or at least, you can't just turn it off or shut the computer). The reason I require this is because auto-play[8] or our own lack of attention will often tempt us to jump right to the next thing. This might be another show or another activity, but sitting and watching the credits is where your mind and heart begin to pro-cess; it's where you turn to the person beside you and say, "So what did you think?"

So much of formation happens after the fact, as we pro-cess together what we saw or experienced. So in the fight over screentime and who forms who, one of the most valuable things we can do for our children is simply sit down for a couple of minutes and talk about what we saw.

---

8. This is low-hanging fruit: turn off auto-play on every device and every network you have and you will never regret it.

Do Not Fear

When I was a kid, I watched a lot of TV. And I played even more video games. So much so that around the time when I was ten years old, my dad told me he would pay me $500 not to watch TV for a year. This was basically an infinite amount of money, so I agreed to do it. There were some exceptions. News was okay to watch—though obviously we didn't care about that one. And sports and movies that the family watched communally were allowed. (I see now my own parents' emphasis on communal watching.) But in general, a new limit was introduced into my life that year, and unsurprisingly, it changed my life.

I remember the feeling while at our grandma's house that I had to go play outside instead of watching Nickelodeon. I remember getting home from school and having to wrestle with boredom and sort it out in the woods instead of in front of the screen. I remember missing video games and being sad when a friend went inside to watch TV and I couldn't come. But I also remember the space that opened up to fall in love with new things: the pleasures of whole afternoons outside with my brothers, extended baseball games in the yard, setting up complicated bike courses on a side street.

I spent a childhood that was, for a long time, pretty tethered to the screen. But then I had an intervening experience.

I mention this, first, because it helps me to see with gracious eyes the mistakes of my own parents: Why did they let me watch *so* much TV?! Why did we have one in all the main rooms of the house, including the kitchen? Why did they buy me every new video game set that I asked for?

But it also helps me see their virtue too. They did what great parents do: they saw their errors and took action. They intervened.

This helps me tremendously when I think about my own generation's journey with screens. Streaming media is barely a decade old, really, and much is rapidly changing. If our goal is not to make mistakes, then we will always feel like failures. And we will give up.

But if our goal is to form our children and help them choose well, that is infinitely more possible *and* infinitely more valuable. That's something we can always do just a little bit better.

This means we approach screentime not with fear but with hope.

Earlier in this chapter I referred to screens as electronic drugs. While I stand by that, I also can tell you that screens are not heroin, where a couple of uses are going to leave you forever changed and addicted. They are more like alcohol. It's serious business and not to be taken lightly. You can handle it much better when you are older and wiser. You need communities of righteousness and wise limitations. Some places it's appropriate; some places it's not.

This is a metaphor that is intended to be put to use. Thinking of screens like we think about the powers, dangers, and pleasures of alcohol helps us realize we have to intervene and make hard decisions. You have to be careful. You have to regulate, because left to our own devices, both screens and alcohol can be extremely dangerous. Imbibing alone regularly (whether from the fount of Jack Daniel's or Netflix) is almost certainly a bad idea, but imbibing occasionally and moderately in community can be rather wonderful.

While children desperately need us to intervene and set good limits for them, they also need us not to be afraid. Note that the Bible never tells us to be fearful of the world, but it often tells us to wake up to it. We would do well to apply that biblical wisdom to screens. We don't make our best decisions out of fear; we make our best decisions out of love. So we do not need to be anxious and worry our days away over the problem of screens, but we do need to wake up to their power. The battle over screentime is the battle for formation of our kids. The fight is worth it, and your best tool is curation.

HABITS OF SCREENTIME
FORMING CHILDREN

Main Idea

The fight for screentime is the fight for formation. But getting rid of screens is not the solution, curation is. This means choosing rhythms that function as limits and then choosing good content to fill those limits.

Adopting Expected Rhythms of On and Off Time Are Ways to Limit Screens

Your rhythms may be different than other people's and may vary in seasons.

Expectations to have:

- Expect others to push back on these ideas, but know that this is important, and stand your ground. Also expect a detox period where your children (and you) act and feel worse when screens are taken away, but know that God made us to be resilient, and this will resolve.

Conversations to have:

- Talk through rhythms with your spouse—a family has to be on the same page about this.
- Once you decide your on/off norms, have a conversation with your kids about what they are and why you're adopting them.

Things to try for on times:

- Weekly family movie nights, Saturday morning cartoons, one night a week, bad/sick days.

Things to try for off times:

- Typical car rides, the dinner table, alone in bedrooms. Consider having one room the family gathers in that does not have a TV or computer. Consider excluding screens from your sabbath rhythms, or if you exclude them other times in the week, consider having them be a special thing you do engage in on the sabbath.

> *"The fight over screentime is a fight over who forms who."*

Within Your Limits, Curate by Choosing Well

The second half of curation is picking well within your limits.

Considerations for picking well:

- Check out "Lauren's Lists" on the website. She has curated lists of shows, movies, video games, and books at https://www.habitsofthehousehold.com/laurenslists.
- Share lists with family and friends of great things to watch.
- Keep lists of creative video or computer games, especially multiplayer ones.
- Consider watching with your kids sometimes, and let shared content become conversation starters.
- Turn off auto-play! Don't let algorithms choose for you.
- Don't be afraid of repeating quality content.
- Consider that quality content is not always free, and good content may be worth the cost.

Remember, though fighting to limit screentime may be one of the hardest sacrifices for us as parents, it is potentially one of the most important things we can do to help our kids thrive and grow into the people God created them to be.

Further Resources

The Tech-Wise Family: Everyday Steps for Putting Technology in Its Proper Place, Andy Crouch
My Tech-Wise Life: Growing Up and Making Choices in a World of Devices, Amy Crouch and Andy Crouch
The Wisdom Pyramid: Feeding Your Soul in a Post-Truth World, Brett McCracken

Remember, grace means it's never too late to start. Don't worry about what your screen practices have been; think about what they could be.

A Note on Adapting

Our rhythms, limits, and values will all look different, but our heart to shepherd our kids should be united. Think about one place where you are surrendering formation to screens, and then try a new habit.

We Always Need the Reminder of Grace: God's love inspires our action, but our action does not inspire God's love. Our family habits will not change God's love for us, but God's love for us should change our family habits.

CHAPTER 5

FAMILY DEVOTIONS

One evening a couple of years ago, I was over at my friend Steve's house and I noticed a book of family devotions on his kitchen table. I picked it up and quickly flipped through a few pages.

"This any good?" I asked him.

He shrugged. "Not sure yet." And then he paused. "But to be honest, I feel like it doesn't really matter. What seems to matter is whether we are doing something or doing nothing." The wisdom of friends.

When it comes to family spiritual formation, it's not about perfect practice, it's about moving from nothing to something.

Doing Something Rather Than Nothing

A couple of months before, Steve and his wife, Lindsay, sat with Lauren and me in a parenting seminar where Don Everts (the author I mentioned earlier) presented research on what makes families spiritually vibrant. As our kids played on the playground outside, we spent part of the workshop doing an assessment of where our families were on certain categories like hospitality, conversation, eating together, and more.

Lauren and I were proud of some things, but the main take-away for us was a convicting epiphany: we realized that the birth of our fourth son had disrupted our former routine of having a family devotional night. It had been years now and we had never gone back to it. Both of us felt the conviction to try to move back to something after a long season of nothing.

That Wednesday, after dinner, I announced that we were going to start our family time Bible studies again. (Never underestimate the power of an announcement to kick off a new rhythm or habit. Naming things matters.)

"Here is what we're going to do," I said. "You all help us clear the table, then we're going to set out a special snack, and we can read a story together."

To my surprise, they were thrilled. Why? Because snacks!

As it turns out, people tend to communicate best while occupying their hands with something else. We stir our tea, hold our coffee, refill our wine, crack our seeds, dip our bread, puff our cigars, peel our oranges, or pit our cherries. We toss a ball, knit a scarf, darn a sock, pluck a guitar, or poke at a fire. Most of our great moments of conversation come when there is something either mindless or tasty sitting in the middle of two people—I call these "third things." We will come back to third things in the chapter on conversation. For now, suffice it to say that interviews and interrogations happen over empty tables. Conversations happen over messy ones. So the beginning of family devotions is just that—a crowded, messy table.

Once the snack was out, I had their relative attention. Let me emphasize the word *relative*. If what we expect at family devotions is a table of quiet children who give us their wide and curious eyes, speak out their Sunday school answers in sweet voices when called on, and then fold their hands and wait their turn to pray, well—you'll be waiting your whole life for family devotions. If our goal was to do something perfect, we'd still be doing nothing. But that is not the goal; the goal is just to do something, and a messy something is still something.

That night, we read a verse together, and I asked them some questions. I can't remember what they were. I'm betting my kids don't either. But what I do know is that ever since, we've been doing the same thing every Wednesday night.

Now, Wednesday nights will, by habit, find us at a messy table still littered with bits of dinner and filling up with crumbs of new snacks. Sometimes we create spaces on the table to put a piece of coloring paper where they will draw what Lauren and I are talking about. Sometimes they follow along in a picture Bible. Sometimes we try memorizing a verse or line of a catechism together. Often, I or Lauren will try to teach some basic truth or just read from a devotional. Always we give them a chance to ask questions about what we read or life or anything else. Always we try to end with each person saying a short prayer about something. Always it's loud and halting and messy, but there's something to that.

In the story of God, messy things are things still worth loving, and that is worth dwelling on for a moment.

Grace Means God Can Love Messy Things

For many parents, there is nothing more intimidating than the idea of reading the Bible or praying together. The fear of how this will happen, and what exactly will happen, is what often keeps anything from happening at all. What will we say? Will we be embarrassed? We don't really know what to teach or talk about. Often this fear of the mess is what keeps us stuck in nothing.

But consider that perhaps what our kids need most is to see us fumble through something. What if the search for the perfect, well-behaved, and well-planned family devotions was undermining one of the key formational aspects of your family? The space to share a mess and proclaim that God loves messy things like us. What if this core truth was the very thing that you are modeling for your children during family devotions?

To dwell on this point, consider some stories from Jesus' life.

Jesus and Messy Kids

There is a remarkable passage retold in Matthew and Luke about parents bringing their kids to Jesus.[1] I love this story, first of all, for the earnest desire of the parents. They must have thought Jesus was really something because they just desperately wanted him to touch their children. To just say a word. To just get close. I like to imagine the part of them that is parents at their best: that part of us that quietly yearns to have our children experience some bit of God, because we know that a bit of God is enough to change anyone.

But I also imagine that this scene cannot have been an orderly line of parents shuffling silent children to the front for a solemn hand of blessing on their forehead. The Luke account notes that the parents were bringing kids—even infants!—which likely meant what you think it means: they were filling the scene with kids who couldn't stop crying and couldn't behave and couldn't wait in line and so on. This was probably a loud and disorderly affair, and the kids must have been participating, because Jesus didn't say, "Let the adults bring the children to me." He said, "Let the children come to me." Apparently, they wanted to. And that signals the reality underneath this passage that is so remarkable. Jesus is actually approachable. He must have even been likable.

---

1. Matt. 19:13–15; Luke 18:15–17.

I'm not sure what to think about first-century kids, but my best guess is that they are like the regular ones we have now. They probably wanted to crawl on Jesus and pull his hair, maybe his earlobe. This is probably why the disciples thought that everyone needed to get back to the serious business.

But Jesus apparently liked the kids better. Jesus probably made funny noises and stuck out his tongue at them. More likely than not he crossed his eyes at them and told a joke, said a brief prayer with a smile, and then poked them in the belly when they were least ready for it in order to catch a giggle.

The gospel writers knew enough to know that this thing he kept doing with kids was significant enough to include it in their accounts, but not wanting to write all the immature details, they seemed to have reduced it to "What can we say? He kept turning the teaching sessions into a daycare."

And don't forget all this applies to adults too. Remember the story Jesus told just before this in Luke 18 about the two men who tried to pray?[2] One walked confidently to the front of the temple and thanked God for lots of things that were so good about himself, while the other stood in the back, unsure of how the worship service was supposed to go, and instead just looked down, beat his chest, and begged for help.

It was the one in the back whose life was a mess who went home not just forgiven but exalted! Because as it turns out, God loves messy things. Really.

He loves broken people. He loves earnest half efforts that don't look right to everyone else. God is crazy about loud children (and self-conscious adults) who don't exactly know how to do the worship thing right but come and give it a shot anyway,

---

2. Luke 18:10–14.

because they know that some little bit of God is better than the nothing they have.

This is what Christians call grace. And grace is the church at its best, the AA of spirituality: Sinners Anonymous, where the only thing you have to show off is your scars. The only ticket that gets you in is the list of reasons you should be kicked out.

Understanding grace in the story of God means that we understand that our mess doesn't stand in the way of connecting with God, it is the means by which we connect with God. Hiding our mess always ends up meaning we hide from God. But bringing our mess to Jesus is the beginning of faith.

This has practical application for messy hearts and messy tables.

Getting Comfortable with the Mess

When it comes to spiritual formation and the family, the reality of grace should free us to approach God without fancy plans or self-consciousness. It reminds us that moving from something to nothing is something that God honors, not rejects.

But where do you start, now that you are comfortable with the mess? There are many places: Read a Bible story out of a picture book at the table. Memorize a verse together. Have a short prayer you say at a certain time of the day. Listen to Scripture in songs so you memorize it. Do a prayer time after dinner once a week. Buy a family devotions book and read it before bed, or before breakfast, or whenever your family is the most in tune to that kind of thing. Have times when kids can ask questions. Follow your kids' Sunday school curriculum and ask them questions about it sometimes on Sunday evenings.

All of these are wonderful items on the menu of family devotions. But you can't, and shouldn't, order it all at one time. Like eating at a good restaurant, you'd be sick if you did that.

What's far better is just to pick one thing. And if you have to pick one thing to go to over and over, you can't go wrong with simple truths or short prayers.

Simple Things: The Truths of the Bible

The most radical truths are really simple ones.

God is real. He loves you. Good and evil exist. Good will win. You are made in the image of God. You are also fallen. Jesus died for you. He also rose for you. God's world is beautiful. We are tasked with caring for it. Men and women exist. Families happen when they unite. Families are like building blocks of a healthy world; we should try to keep them together, and not topple them over. Prayer is real; it changes you as much as it changes the world. Life is hard, but God is with you. Suffering will happen, but it will sanctify you. Love is not a feeling, it is a sacrifice, usually in small things. God loves you, period. Your good deeds won't change that; your bad deeds won't change that. I will never leave you. Neither will Mom.

These are the life-altering paradigms that come in just a couple of words, once every Wednesday night. The rest of the week is about living them out, yes, but how powerful is it to find a moment in the week to just say one of them out loud?

We do great battle against lies when we do this, because just as the most significant truths are the simplest ones, so the most dangerous lies are the same way: evil doesn't really exist, you aren't really lovable, your parents might leave, no one hears your prayers, you are essentially alone, things don't happen for a reason, your body doesn't matter, you are a cosmic accident, you have to fight to earn your place in the world, no one's going to help you.

These seeds of lies are as small as they are harmful. And when they take root in the mind, they can grow and crack the foundation of any child's head and heart. So it is the job of a parent to constantly supplant them by teaching the simple and wonderful truths of God's Word, over and over.

Leaning on Catechisms

If you suddenly feel that you have to come up with a master plan of family devotions to cover all the essential areas of simple truths, there is good news for you: *no one has to do this.* We are—praise God!—part of a historic, global church family who over thousands of years has refined incredible and beautiful ways to help parents like you and me think about how to start teaching our children. They are called catechisms.[3]

Picture catechisms like the first set of building blocks a kid gets. They're simple wooden blocks, but they're sturdy and they'll stay in the family for generations.

Catechisms (intentionally) play on the unique ability of children to memorize things. Here are the first few questions in one that we have used. And note that Coulter, at three years old, for example, could say all this with us:

> **Parent:** Who made you?
> **Child:** God.
> **Parent:** What else did God make?
> **Child:** All things.
> **Parent:** Why did God make all things?
> **Child:** For his own glory.[4]

---

3. See a few recommended resources at the end of this chapter if you need a place to start.
4. Beginning of Catechism for Young Children. You can find a link to this in the resources section.

Not only is it ridiculously cute to hear a three-year-old say, "Fowr his oown gwory," it's a phenomenal gift to them. It plants the seeds of the idea that God is good, he made us, he's worth worshiping.

Catechisms at a young age work like holds in a rock-climbing wall. They are sturdy things a mind can grab hold of and begin to work with.

Short Things: The Gift of Prayer

If the simple truths of the Bible are the way God talks to us, the other side of that coin is teaching our children to talk back to God. This is prayer. For kids, this means short prayers.

One of the things I try to do each time my side of our extended family does a family vacation is take each of the boys on a one-on-one outing. One summer when we were at the beach, I took Ash out to get some donuts when, tragically, we got lost. I thought I remembered the donut place from the last year when we went to the same beach, but I didn't bring a phone and I was wrong.

For ten to fifteen minutes, we drove up and down the main road with me mumbling, "I'll recognize it when I see it, Ash. I'll recognize it."

Finally, and fortunately, it proved true. When I whipped the minivan into the lot, fist pumping, Ash quietly said, "Papa, I knew we would find it."

"Oh, you did?" I asked.

"Yeah. Because I prayed we would." He said it confidently, then added, "Like five times."

I didn't know whether to laugh or cry or ask questions to nuance his approach to prayer. My first thought was, "Does he think God is a vending machine for donuts? What would have happened if he prayed and I didn't find it? Does he think the number of times he asks matters?"

I was about to ask some of these questions when, probably because of the good work of the Holy Spirit, I stopped and thought, "Do I want a kid who brings his small things to God without self-consciousness? Earnestly enough to count the number of his prayers? Or do I want a kid who thinks his stuff is not important enough for God, so he just doesn't pray at all?"

As it was, I just smiled and said, "I'm so glad, Ash. God answered your prayer."

Does Ash think that God is a vending machine for donuts? Maybe, I don't know. We'll get there. But if he did, would that be all that different from my struggle to think that God is a vending machine for my job, health, and happiness? My desires aren't more noble just because they're older. We all struggle with trying to get what we want from God, rather than realizing what we want is simply him.

As it was, that morning I admired Ash. Even envied him. I want to be a child like that. I want to go back to when I came to Jesus in short, earnest prayers and let him sort out the rest.

I somehow forget over and over that Jesus tells us to come to him like children do.[5] Full of simple desires and short words. No pretenses.

I remember when my parents gave the gift of short prayers to me. I was six and I was terrified to go to bed every night. They highlighted a verse in my Bible and told me to take it to bed and pray it. It is at the tip of my tongue still now. Thirty-some years later, I type from memory: "Thou wilt keep him in perfect peace, whose mind is stayed on thee: because he trusteth

---

5. Matt. 18:3.

in thee" (KJV).[6] Never mind the King James translation. Never mind that I was a six-year-old who didn't know what "stayed" meant. There was something much more fundamental at work, a simple truth contained in a short prayer—God is with you when you're scared. You're not alone, and you can think about him.

I still remember saying it softly to myself, head on the pillow when no one else was awake. It came with me to camp when I was terrified of being away. It came with me on sleepovers when I was lonely. The echoes of that young spiritual epiphany have continued to grow over the years. Now when I'm in the middle of my "adult" anxiety and fears, head on the pillow and mind spinning, a promise that was set in motion decades ago renews itself again and again: He is with me here in this fear. My mind can dwell on him. I trust in him. Peace is possible.

We shouldn't make complicated work out of teaching our kids to pray. When Jesus taught us to pray, he gave us something short and met us where we were. Pray about bread. Pray about being delivered. Call God your father. Over and over in Scripture, Jesus tells us that the short, earnest prayers are the real ones, and the long, flowery ones are masquerading as religion trying to earn God's attention when all he wants is a desperate heart.

When we do family prayer in the morning, when I invite a child to pray with me by the bedside, when we pray before dinner, or when I ask them to pray after family devotions, it always has one thing in common: *brevity*. It's real, but it's short.

Often Whit, when he's really hungry, mischievously asks if he can pray before dinner. I know what he's going to say, but I say yes anyway. He goes: "God thank you amen!" And digs

---

6. Isa. 26:3.

in. I think it's a good joke, and not a bad prayer either, because God loves short things, and simple things, and messy things. And that's how life actually happens, and that is where prayer is taught.

Teaching our kids to pray is a work done mostly on the fly. Less in the pews and at Sunday school tables and more in the back seats of cars and the ends of grocery lines. Over skinned knees and missed catches. If we want our children to grow up and want God instead of the things he gives, we might start by teaching them that he's an approachable God; he's a warm, smiling father who won't send them away for immaturity. God himself is worth wanting to be with.

When Toddlers Pray

One night after family devotions, we asked if Coulter had any questions about what we read from the devotions. He was so short in his chair that his head barely rose above the table. He frowned, leaned his chin on the table, and said, "Ummmm. My brothers keep bothering me, and I praise God for the swimming pool."

He was barely three at the time. We are used to toddler nonsense, but this seemed to be more than that. We all stared in silent confusion until Lauren all at once realized what was happening.

"Those are his prayer requests!" she proclaimed with the triumph that often follows a toddler-babble epiphany. "He wants God's help with what to do when his brothers bother him, and he is thankful for swimming. Is that right, Coulter?"

He rested his head on his hands and sighed like it was obvious: "Yeah . . ." If he had known the word *duh*, he would have used it.

That's when it hit me that this tiny-brained three-year-old was in a rhythm of sharing prayer requests. Even though he got the prompt wrong (we were asking if he had any questions), the instinct was remarkable. He expected to be asked what to pray for, and even when we didn't ask, he was ready to answer it. "What do I need God to help me with? What am I thankful to him for?" These were questions we asked all the time, and that night they were on his mind before we asked.

Before we moved from nothing to something, I wouldn't have expected that with a few times of just showing up to family devotions, a three-year-old's mind and heart could be adapted to rhythms of prayer.

But like the rest of us, children are hungry for patterns and will pick up on them. Which is why it's worth picking the right patterns and not settling for the default ones.

Thankfully, those patterns don't have to be complicated. Because the most powerful truths are the simplest ones, the most enduring prayers are the shortest ones, the places where these patterns unfold are the messy ones, and God loves messy things.

HABITS OF FAMILY DEVOTIONS
FORMING CHILDREN

Main Idea

When it comes to family devotions, it is not about perfect practice, it is about doing something rather than nothing. Grace means that God loves small, messy things like us and our kids. Making a habit of teaching simple truths and praying short prayers is one of the smallest and most powerful rhythms a family can practice.

Ideas for Moving from Something to Nothing

God loves messy things. You are not trying to create a perfect moment, or even teach a well-planned lesson. You are just trying to create moments where you, and your children, wrestle with Scripture and pray out loud and together.

- Look for times where you are already gathered (such as breakfast or dinner).
- Try reading a short verse together a couple of times to memorize it.
- Try reading a story from a children's book and then each sharing one thing you liked about it (you don't need to corner your kids into saying things adults think are spiritual—letting them process Scripture with you is meaningful in its own right).
- End with each person saying a one-sentence prayer about something they need, or are thankful for, or are happy about—making sure to affirm children's things to pray about, and not needlessly correct their prayer to something that is more mature than they can understand.
- Feel free to process in front of them, noting things you wonder about the passage or God. Children absorb the way we think, so just being sincere and open in front of them is a kind of teaching of its own.

Remember, God has always taught his church through broken sinners. Your hard day or recent failure doesn't disqualify you from teaching grace—it disqualifies you from teaching moralism. Start with repentance and confession, and you'll always end up pointing to Jesus.

> *"The most radical truths are simple ones. The most genuine prayers are short ones."*

Telling Simple Truths and Praying Short Prayers

Things to try for telling simple truths:

- Try reading or memorizing some lines of a catechism together. (Try New City Catechism, this catechism for young children (http://sovgraceto.org/wp-content/uploads/2012/02/Catechism-for-Young-Children.pdf), or, for older children, The Westminster Shorter Catechism.) Starting with one question-and-response a week is ideal.
- Go through the Lord's Prayer or the Apostles' Creed and explain the concepts. Again, one line a week is plenty of fodder.
- If you do family mottos, try basing one around a short passage of Scripture (e.g., We Try to Be Strong and Courageous or We Try to Be Joyful Always).
- Memorize Scripture through music (Slugs & Bugs combines Scripture with really great music that you'll enjoy too).

Things to try for praying short prayers:

- Pray together when you find yourselves in need.
- Invite them to pray before a meal.
- Pray for them, out loud, when they share something they feel or need.
- Consider praying together before school or bedtime (see the bedtime chapter for examples).
- Pray together after a fight in the family happens.

Further Resources

DEVOTIONS

Teach Us to Pray: Scripture-Centered Family Worship through the Year, Lora A. Copley and Elizabeth Vander Haagen (This is the single-best resource we've found for incorporating both younger and older children in devotions.)

What Every Child Should Know about Prayer, Nancy Guthrie (ages four and up)

Foundations: Twelve Biblical Truths to Shape a Family, Ruth Chou Simons and Troy Simons (for whole-family devotions, ages eight and up)

The Ology: Ancient Truths Ever New, Marty Machowski (ages six and up)

Indescribable: 100 Devotions about God and Science, Louie Giglio (ages six and up)

CATECHISMS

New City Catechism, adapted by Timothy Keller and Sam Shammas

Catechism for Young Children: An Introduction to the Shorter Catechism (This is the best resource we've found for young children, two and up. You can view a version online at https://reformed.org/historic-confessions/the-childrens-catechism.)

The Westminster Shorter Catechism

BIBLES

The Jesus Storybook Bible, Sally Lloyd-Jones (ages two and up)

The Action Bible, Doug Mauss and Sergio Cariello (ages five and up)

My First Hands-On Bible, Tyndale House (ages two to five)

A Note on Adapting

Age and stage will matter tremendously for figuring out what family Scripture and prayer looks like. Consider some of the following movements, as kids age:

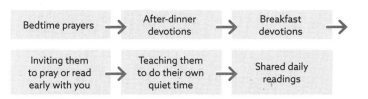

We Always Need the Reminder of Grace: God's love inspires our action, but our action does not inspire God's love. Our family habits will not change God's love for us, but God's love for us should change our family habits.

CHAPTER 6

MARRIAGE

On Wednesday night, the week feels too long and too short all at once. We're far enough into things to feel tired and busy, but still too far from the weekend to feel like the work is close to being over. There's too much left to do, the mess in the house is starting to build up, and we feel like we need to catch up. And yet, it is here amid the middle-of-life-mood of a Wednesday night that Lauren and I put the kids to bed and stop everything.

We don't open the computers to work. We don't finish the laundry. We don't follow up on the kids' doctor appointments. We don't do any of the things we're "supposed" to do, because Wednesday night is date night.

There is a strange paradox here: in date night, all the work of the household is ignored so we can focus on the one thing that keeps the household working—marriage.

It is a terrible fiction to imagine we can be good mothers and fathers without being good husbands and wives. In the story of God, the strength of the household depends on the strength of marriage. It may be the most practical—and the most profound—thing we do. So we pause here in the middle of this book to talk about the habit that holds all of the other habits together—the habit of covenant love.

Marriage and the Biblical Importance of Covenant Love

The story of the world begins, and ends, in a wedding.[1]

At the beginning, there are words and light, song and rest, fruit and animals, yes. But center stage in all of that is the union of the first bride and groom. Almost as if everything else was the processional, the characters funneling in, taking their seats, and waiting for the big moment. The stage of creation is set for a ceremony—man meets woman. There is suspense—man comes out on stage and God says, "You are alone. This is not good!" Then there is the great reveal—"Here is the bride!" And in the moment that man and woman behold each other, creation sings, and so does Adam. There is poetry and wonder, bone and flesh, and the promise of new life. Marriage is the beginning of this whole story.

But marriage is the end of the story too. At the end of time, there are fire and clouds, suns and moons, trees and new cities, but again, it is all mostly the clatter and bang for another ceremony, bigger this time. This is no intimate garden party, this is a cosmic celebration, because the war is over and peace has been won. The kingdom gathers and it's time for the king and queen to get married. This is the marriage of God to his people, the church and the church's lover, always smitten and now finally united.

So it is that the arc of Scripture bends from wedding to wedding, and God's covenant love connects them.

Marriage, then, is not *a* great theme of Scripture. It is *the*

---

1. Herman Bavinck, *The Christian Family* (1908).

great theme of Scripture. Covenant love is the gravity that gives shape to the whole of the narrative.

It's important to define this term, *covenant love*. There are two meanings of the word *love* as we typically use it: the first is a feeling, the second is a covenant.

First, love as a feeling. This is the meaning we use the most, though it is really just selfishness disguised as love. This is the kind of love that says, "I love you because of how you make me feel." But if this is what love means, then really we love someone only because of what we get out of it. Love as a feeling is conditional and predicated on a sense of individual freedom: "I'll love you, so long as it makes me happy, but then I'm free to leave."

The second use is totally different: that is love as a promise, or covenant love. Covenant love is completely the opposite of love as a feeling. Covenant love says, "I love you despite what it costs me." This, of course, is the biblical story of love. God loves his bride, the church, despite all our foolishness and adultery. "Though it may undo me," he says in Jesus, "I will love you." This is love as an action, a commitment where individual freedom is surrendered so that love can flourish. This is why marriage vows say, "In sickness or in health, for richer or for poorer, for better or for worse, till death do us part."

And as it turns out, paradoxically, it is the love that says, "I'll love you despite how I feel" that leads to freedom and happiness.

So it is that covenant love is one of the most important things that the school of love will teach. When we practice covenant love, we teach our kids that love is not something you stop practicing just because you stop feeling like it. No, love is something you finally feel because you keep practicing it. It's by acting like people in love that we become people in love. Not vice versa.

We stop here in the middle of the book to consider marriage because the school of love is predicated on parents acting out covenant love. But take heart, this is not as destined for failure as it sounds. Acting out covenant love does not mean pretending marriage is easy. It is the opposite; it means admitting that marriage is hard and trying anyway. And in that struggle, you are not alone. All of us as husbands and wives are struggling to love each other well.

If you haven't had a really hard season in your marriage yet, it will come. It is the norm, not the exception. But marriage being really hard is not a sign that you are failing, it is a sign that marriage is working. Loving someone despite all their flaws and despite all your flaws is supposed to be hard and sanctifying work. It is one of the ways we become more like Christ.[2] This is why we make a habit of practicing the covenant.

Date Night as a Habit of Rehearsing the Covenant

As a practice, date night is simple enough. You set aside an evening for each other somewhere in the week (whether in or out of the house) and you stick to it. You know you will be too busy and too tired, but that's why you schedule it.

Maybe you watch a movie, or maybe you schedule an evening out. Maybe you cook together or maybe you read to each other. Perhaps you take a walk or you sit down with a glass of wine. Whatever you do, you must know that it will go wrong as often as it goes right. You hoped for conversation, but you're fighting instead. You had great dinner reservations, but the kids got sick. You ordered takeout, but one of you is mad because it blew the budget. You hoped for something romantic, but as it turns out, he keeps checking the score or she keeps checking her phone.

It is never quite the way it was supposed to be. But you try

---

2. Eph. 5:21–27.

anyway. Because that's not just the story of date night, that's the story of marriage. Sinners trying to love each other never turns out like we thought, but we keep going because we made a covenant.

In this sense, the seemingly simple pattern of weekly date night is something much more powerful: it is a way of rehearsing that covenant.

Early on in our marriage, Lauren and I were advised to set aside time each week to spend with each other. We took the advice even though early in marriage it seemed a bit silly. At that point we spent all our time together anyway; why focus on a certain night? But in retrospect, it is now all the more obvious. Because we spent all of our time together, we needed to set aside time and space that was special and intentional, lest it all became one blurred and monotonous string of being together. Now it is a bit the opposite. If we didn't carve out a date night each week, we would never see each other. There is way too much else going on. So both in times of surplus and deficit, date night plays the same role: we come together to create a different kind of space for marriage.

For us, often this is simply putting the phones away and sitting on the couch after bedtime and having a glass of wine or a cocktail together. Maybe it's dessert, just to make the night feel special. Once in a while it's watching a movie together. Maybe once a month it is getting a sitter and going out for dinner or drinks. But always it is trying to make time and space to find each other in conversation or laughter. Always it is trying to make time for sex. Always it is trying to make sure we are checking in emotionally and finding some way to say that we are more than parents: we are co-laborers, we are friends, we are lovers.

As mentioned, this does not always have to be out of the house. And it certainly doesn't have to require spending money. There are so many ways to create that space for marriage inside the house. At the same time, I think it is helpful to note the importance of getting comfortable with babysitters so that you can get out of the house regularly.

Kids demand attention, constantly. But one of the central things that we need in our marriage is to give, and get, the undivided attention of our spouse. Yes, we are parents, but first we are husband and wife. And if we do not work to do well as husband and wife, our work of parenting will be in vain. You can't teach love without embodying it.

So there should be a premium value in parenting on having time where you can remove yourself from parenting. Parenting is really hard work, and like all work, we need a break from it to do it well. That is why childcare is so valuable to marriage. This may be family watching for free, this may be friends whose kids you'll also take a turn watching, this may be older children watching younger ones, or this may be hired help[3]—whatever it is, you are going to need to either spend money or relational capital to make it work. And I want you to know that it is worth the expense because that spending reveals the value you place on your marriage.

But whether we hire a babysitter or not, the point of date night is that we make a habit of coming together without the kids.

As is the thesis of this book, our greatest moments of meaning are hidden in the ordinary ones. Without the monotonous rhythm of Wednesday night date nights, I wouldn't know what Lauren really thought about that headline, she wouldn't know

---

3. Note that regularly having other people watch your kids is good for them and good for the household too. It helps diffuse the illusion that you and you alone can protect your kids, that you alone can teach your kids, that you alone are the best thing for your kids. It acknowledges the reality that we all need help. This is healthy to acknowledge. Even more, it allows your children the blessing of learning from and understanding different types of authority and friendship. Bonding with aunts or family friends, with grandparents or babysitters is a particularly useful skill and a wonderful reinforcement of the idea that the orbit of the household circles many people.

what I really felt about what happened with Shep earlier that week, she would have no idea what I was dreaming about or worried about at work, and I wouldn't know her greatest hopes for the consulting project she was just staffed on, or why she is so frustrated with that text I sent. But in regular rhythms of coming together, we don't just find these things out, we find each other.

Habitually Giving the Gift of Time Alone

One of the themes of this book is acknowledging how hard parenting is. It is an incredibly difficult task that demands everything of us almost all of the time, which is why one of the greatest gifts we can give our spouse is a break from being a parent—some time alone.

One of the gifts of marriage is that we can do this for each other in regular rhythms. For example, where Wednesday night is date night, Tuesday night is boys' night. It's the night I say to Lauren, "Get out of the house. Go work on your computer, go see a friend, go buy yourself dinner, go shop, go drive, go sit, go stare at the sky, or just go do whatever else it is you need to do to feel like a regular human being again." It is impossible to underestimate what a gift this is to a parent who is at home all day with the kids. The gift of silence might be the best prayer time they have that week. The moment not to think might turn into the most meaningful reflection of their year.

As husband and wife, one of the things we commit to is helping the other become holy, not just happy.[4] Part of this is remembering that you are not just a parent, and relating to God as a full human being. This should not wait until our kids are

---

4. "Husbands, love your wives, just as Christ loved the church and gave himself up for her to make her holy, cleansing her by the washing with water through the word, and to present her to himself as a radiant church, without stain or wrinkle or any other blemish, but holy and blameless" (Eph. 5:25–27).

grown, this should happen as a regular habit for both parents, and marriage is uniquely suited to provide that.

Habits of Showing Affection

To be the best father I can be to my boys, I want them to see my commitment to loving Lauren. Much of this they won't understand when they are young, but just because they don't understand everything does not mean they don't notice everything. There is no hiding from your family; kids notice everything, though they may interpret it later.

They see how I talk to her when I'm tired. They see how I hug her in the morning. They listen when we're short with each other. They watch when we're cold to each other. They notice if we hold hands while we're driving, and they also notice when we snap at each other while we're loading the car. They watch the way we say "I love you" and the way we say "I'm sorry."

For example, I thought one of our great moments of parenting was one morning when I said something short and impatient to Lauren just because I was frustrated about being late to work. All the boys were in the kitchen. "Don't be rude to me just because you're mad," she said firmly. And she was right. I got to apologize, right then and there in front of everyone, and she got to forgive me and kiss me to prove it. I was so glad for that moment.

As you have read, one of the things I tell my boys most nights is that I will love them no matter what they do. I promise them regularly that I will never leave them. But they are kids, and while words are really important, they are definitively not as important as the life I live in front of them. When I love Lauren in front of them, I'm proving it.

When I act out the covenant of marriage in our family, I teach the boys that love is real in a way that words alone cannot teach. And they need that. At best, they watch us work on love. They watch us reconcile when we mess up and act out love even when we don't feel like it.

These things can be made into habits, though the prescriptions may be different, depending on what is natural for your marriage. Perhaps it is kissing when one of you comes home. Perhaps it is always speaking well of each other in front of the kids. Perhaps it is committing to saying sorry publicly if you fought publicly. Perhaps it is telling stories to your kids about why you love your spouse so much. In this kind of thing, you'll invent your habits better than anyone else can. Just remember that the little things you habitually do in front of your kids is an enormous part of the marriage legacy you leave them, and that's not a burden, that's a gift and an opportunity.

The Habit of Parenting Check-Ins

Occasionally, during a date night or some other set-aside time, Lauren and I will have a parenting check-in. There is no formula to this, it is simply a set-aside time where we ask each other: What are the kids going through? How are we responding? What do we feel good about? What do we feel guilty about? How can we accept God's grace for that guilt, and how can we lean into his call for what we should do better?

These moments are inevitably so valuable for us both. We are often so in the fray that she might not know that I had an important conversation with Ash, or I might not know that she read a good book that would help us on discipline, or that we were both thinking differently about how to handle Coulter's age and stage. For us, parenting check-ins are part fun, part hard, part interesting, and part challenging.

Usually they are planned in advance. For example, we will

agree that next date night we'll make our conversation a parenting check-in. Usually we bring a journal so we can write things down and look at what we wrote down last time. And usually we'll try to pray or commit to praying about something we talked about. But aside from that, it is nothing more than simply creating space to talk about how we are doing.

The Habit of Dreaming Together

One of my favorite things to do with Lauren, whether on a date night or a vacation or a long car ride, is to ask what she is thinking about for the future and to tell her what I'm thinking about. There is a range of questions here. What friend does she wish she were closer to? What is she hoping for in returning to work? What is broken that we need to fix in our patterns? What is a goal she is hoping for or working toward? Where does she feel our family is headed? What can we do about that? Hopefully, I'll respond with mine or she'll ask too.

At best, these are questions that try to understand something that is not necessarily on the surface of the relationship: What are you hoping for? What are you dreaming of? And this is so important because if we miss the dreams of our spouse, or misunderstand them, we almost guarantee grudges and pain and fights. Life is hard enough as it is, and one way to come together is to at least know what your spouse is dreaming of and what they are hoping for. That is the beginning of dreaming with them and fighting for them.

Finding Jesus through Marriage

In the end, all of this business about practicing the covenant is just one way of saying that we're trying to love each other like Jesus loves us. Which is a radical thing.

The unconditional love of Jesus means that no matter what we've done or left undone, he loves us and he is making us new anyway. It is on this foundational promise of grace that we can have the courage to make promises to our family.

To be clear, these are fearsome promises. In the covenant of marriage, we promise to stare death and loss in the face and love each other anyway. We promise to look into the abyss and, trembling, reach out for the other's hand. Marriage is the most silly and beautiful thing we do. Perhaps that is why it makes or breaks everything else we do.

But take heart, because if this seems difficult, remember it is only a holy imitation of our covenant relationship with God. We're not inventing this; we're just dancing to the tune we hear. We're imitating the wedding we see at the end of time. Like marriage, following Jesus is a gamble that asks everything of you. We're responding to the thunderous altar call, to drop everything and come get married to God. In this heavenly gamble, we stake our lives on someone else. We surrender what we have now for what is to come later. We claim that the way up is the way down. We become strangers to the world so we can be friends with God. We admit that we can't find ourselves at all until we find ourselves in him.

Marriage is radical because Christianity is radical, and that is a beautiful thing to display to our children. It's a nod to the God who has loved us into loving. When we rehearse the covenant of marriage in front of them, we rehearse the promise of our own salvation in front of them: God is a God who never gives up on love, so neither will we.

HABITS OF MARRIAGE

FORMING PARENTS

Main Idea

The covenant love of marriage is the foundation of love in the family. Habits of working on covenant love reveals the core truth of the family: binding love sets us free.

Ideas for Making Date Night a Rhythm

Things to try:

- Name a night of the week that will become a regular date night. No matter how informal, make that an intentional evening. If you use a shared calendar, put it on there.
- Don't feel the pressure to make it out of the house, just make undistracted space at home.
- Have a conversation about whether getting more babysitting would be good for your marriage.
- Keep lists of questions for each other; pull them out on conversation evenings (see some examples below).
- Use this date night as a way to regularly connect both physically and emotionally.

Questions for Parenting Check-Ins

- What's going well? What's hard?
- What do you need my help with?
- Who are you connecting well with? Who are you having trouble connecting with?
- How is discipline going?
- How is each child doing developmentally? Academically? Physically? Spiritually? Character development?

- Are we too busy to parent well? Are we too busy as a family?
- How are we pointing our children to Jesus?
- Do we need to apologize for anything?
- Do you need to have a one-on-one talk or an important conversation with a particular child?

> *"The story of the world begins, and ends, in a wedding."*

Questions for Date Night

- What is bringing you joy? What is weighing on you?
- When you picture Jesus looking at you, what is the expression on his face?
- What do you find yourself continually daydreaming about?
- What is one thing I can do to love you better? Encourage you more? Support you better?
- What is one daily or weekly rhythm you want to start? What's one you want to stop?
- What's something you've done recently that you're proud of?
- Who is your closest friend right now? Who do you want to be closer to?
- What are you reading, listening to, or watching that's interesting?

Ideas for Gifting Alone Time

- Regular night when one parent does dinner and bedtime solo (so the other can get out of the house or just relax).
- Weekends away with guy- or girlfriends.
- Saturday morning outings with just one parent.
- If one parent has to travel, try giving the other parent some time off when you come back.

Further Resources

ON MARRIAGE

The Meaning of Marriage: Facing the Complexities of Commitment with the Wisdom of God, Timothy Keller with Kathy Keller

Two-Part Invention: The Story of a Marriage, Madeleine L'Engle

CONVERSATION STARTERS ON PARENTING AND SPIRITUALITY IN THE HOME

The Domestic Monastery, Ronald Rolheiser (This is a fantastic little book on the spirituality of the home.)

Family Discipleship: Leading Your Home through Time, Moments, and Milestones, Matt Chandler and Adam Griffin (This is a helpful book on discipleship in the home.)

A Note on Adapting

If you're divorced or a single parent, this may be a very difficult chapter. If so, I will not presume to apply it for you. I will only gently encourage you that God's covenant love for you is more real than any of us know, and that is the love that in the end heals all pain.

> **We Always Need the Reminder of Grace:** God's love inspires our action, but our action does not inspire God's love. Our family habits will not change God's love for us, but God's love for us should change our family habits.

CHAPTER 7

WORK

I have this vivid memory as a young child of watching my dad and my uncle Chas work on my dad's motorcycle together. I remember that the garage was painted red and that wrenches littered the floor under the bike. I remember that the 250cc Yamaha motorcycle never worked except about once a year following the couple of days they worked on it. But this was an annual ritual of sorts, and for me, as a kid, it was the place I wanted to be. So I stood off to the side waiting for someone to ask me for help.

When my dad finally looked up and said, "Hey, can you hand me that wrench?" you would have thought I was just drafted into the Major Leagues, asked to be Secretary of State, or hand-selected for the Navy SEALs. I was over the moon because now I was involved. "Which wrench do you need?" I was excited to show that I knew the difference—even though I didn't. Perhaps I could suggest the right one, I wondered, or even give it a half crank. The possibilities were endless.

Deep down in a child is the desire to be included in the work of the person who loves them. My dad loved me. I loved him. And I desperately wanted to be invited into his work.

We may grow up, but we never grow out of this longing to work beside the one who loves us. Because in the story of God, we were made to work.

Work in the Story of God

There is perhaps no simpler way to understand the Genesis call to work than this: We are invited into the work of the God who loves us. We were meant for this. Which is why our work inevitably becomes one of our greatest blessings, or one of our greatest burdens. That's how spiritually important work is.

When we reduce work to a means of income, we take the spiritual dignity out of it, and that will always end up robbing us of some dignity too. This is true whether we're in a season of fulfilling work, hard work, or even no work. How we deal with those blessings or burdens will always be central to our spirituality. So work is not just a way to make the ends of life meet, work is better understood as an end that makes meaning of life.

If work is really that spiritually important, then forming our children in a deep understanding that God created us to work alongside him, and to take pleasure in that work, is paramount to raising a child.

But for many reasons, this is not easy at all. Often, the work we do inside the home is unfairly demoted to "housework," the work we do outside the home is invisible to them, and the rest of the work we do on screens that they can't see or understand.

It would be one thing to wait until our children get to high school and then hand them a book on the theology of work—but why wait when habits of the household can lay so much groundwork in forming a child to understand the spiritual dignity of work, both inside and outside the home?

To do this, we can practice:

1. Habits of talking about work
2. Habits of inviting them into the work of the household
3. Habits of letting them see the work outside the household

1. Practicing Habits of Talking about Work

I remember when Whit was only two years old, we were coming back from an out-of-town Christmas celebration with family and Lauren was going to drop me off at the law firm so I could wrap up some projects before the New Year.

Understandably jarred from having just spent a couple of days' vacation together, Whit whined, "Why do you have to go back to work?"

I was maybe overambitious in my sense of what teaching was possible with a two-year-old; I told him that I didn't *have* to go to work, I *wanted* to go to work. Then, feeling even more spunky, I added, "because God *made* us to work."

Perhaps sensing an imbalance in what Whit was looking for, Lauren turned around in the front seat and added, "But Papa also *has* to go to work because he has a responsibility to work. He doesn't just want to be away from us all the time," she clarified. Finding that to be mostly right, but needing further nuance, I chimed in that "Yes, work is hard and it's not always fun, but it's one of the ways we become more like God, and we shouldn't be sad about work." Lauren then added that was true but not everyone had work, and it was also something to be thankful for.

And now you can see a bit of what our marriage is like. We kept on driving down the highway, nuancing each other's sentences long after Whit had stopped paying attention.

There may have been some wasted words there, but I look back at that moment and think that Lauren and I—as relatively new parents—were exploring the difficult territory of explaining to children why we work. And that's not easy. It's hard enough to explain to ourselves what work is and why we do it. So practicing habits of language helps them *and* reminds us what the big-picture story of work is.

You certainly can't teach a theology of work in one car ride—and fortunately, you don't have to. But you *can* model it over a childhood, and you *can* give your child an inheritance of words by anticipating the usual questions and practicing good answers. Here are some examples of kid-friendly answers that help build a bigger, spiritual picture of work:

- **"Why do you have to go to work today?"**
  - "I *get* to go to work—which I'm actually really thankful for. Because God made us all to work. Some people don't have a job they like, and some don't have a job at all. Work is a blessing."
- **"What do you do at work?"**
  - Just like God helps people, at work I get to help people by . . .
  - Just like God created the world, at work I get to create things, like . . .
  - Just like the Bible tells us to serve other people, at work I get to serve other people by . . .
- **"Why do we have to do chores?"**
  - Just like God organized the world and made it a good place for us to live, it's our job to keep our house organized so it's a good place for us to live.

Let's be clear, your kids will have way more questions, and some of these answers may not land, but again, think of them as seeds you are planting. These conversations unfold over decades.

Of course, there are also many times where work will feel

like much more of a burden than a blessing, but even when we are in those hard times, and maybe especially in those time, we can still give our children a significant gift by modeling dignity in suffering and courage in sadness.

- **In unemployment, we might say:**
  - "God made us to work, so one of the reasons Mom/ Dad is so sad right now is that they don't have a job to go to. It's sad like being really good at riding bikes, but not having one to enjoy it."
- **In underemployment, we might say:**
  - "God made us with special talents and tells us to use them, so one of the reasons Mom/Dad is so sad right now is that their job doesn't use their talents."
- **In hard times of overwork, we might say:**
  - "Just like God works and then rests, one of the reasons it is so hard for Mom/Dad right now is that their job is not letting them rest, and good rest is just as important as good work."

2. Practicing Habits of Inviting Children into the Work of the Household

"Why doesn't Mama work?" Ash once asked me. I could tell by the wide-eyed look on his face that the look on my own face was bordering on rage. "Mama not work?! Are you kidding?" I had to remind myself that he was only four, after all, and he still didn't understand the work that goes into the household. He is also not privy to all of our marital nuances and frustrations about Lauren's career before kids, and how she actually desires to go back to work someday but is just not there yet, and in the meantime is working harder than all of us just by staying home to work.

So I simply said, "Mama does more work than all of us; let me tell you about it."

We had a good talk about the work that it takes to keep a house, and how that work is a loving service to everyone who lives in it, but words are not sufficient for anyone, and certainly not for children.

If they are going to learn work, *they need to be regularly invited into the work of the house.*

This is inevitably messier than it is helpful, at least at first. But how else will they come to understand the satisfaction of a job well done? How will they come to understand the dignity of the work a stay-at-home parent performs? The reason I insist on inviting the boys (or put bluntly, forcing them) into the work of the house is to pull back the curtains and show them that creating a place of hospitality, health, and conversation takes a whole lot of work.

The tough parts about putting kids to work in the house are many and obvious—they mess it up, they complain, they are slow, they need to be constantly monitored, and sometimes you'd much rather just turn on a screen and say, "Fine, I'll clean it up, just don't bother me while I do it." All true and all understandable. But here are some of the less noticed benefits of regularly inviting children into the work of the house.

Unique Quality Time

When I invite them to help prep a meal with me (especially one on one), they get the pleasure I got in the garage. There is a particular bond to helping your parent, and this is a dynamic to nurture and grow. One of our veteran mom friends once told Lauren, "If you do it alone, you'll always do it alone." Though I remember despising being asked to dry dishes as a kid, I now look forward to doing the dishes beside my mom after our Sunday family lunches, because it's a time to talk to her.

We Need the Help

I will not go into the sociology of how the breakdown of extended families is leaving parents more and more alone and how technology is driving more outside work into the home, but suffice it to say that our modern moment leaves parents with as much work as ever with as little help as ever. The last thing we need to add is making our kids' beds and picking up their clothes when they can easily do these things for themselves. When I dump a huge load of laundry on the downstairs table and tell the boys to pick out their clothes, it's not only good for them to learn to put their own clothes away, but it teaches us all that many hands make light work. I'd be there all night wondering whose dino shirt is whose, when they know it instantly.

Teaching Them the Satisfaction of Work

Seeing a child in flow is a wonderful thing. There is an immense satisfaction children get to bringing order to a small realm that they can control. This happens in doing puzzles and coloring pages, but this also really can happen in folding towels, sweeping floors, loading dishwashers, or sorting silverware. If we don't take the time to teach them these things, we rob ourselves of the help, and we rob them of the opportunity to build an early memory of how satisfying a focused and finished task can be.

Teaching Them That Rhythms of Order Are Fundamental to Everything

I'll never forget the summers of my childhood when my mom would wake us up and say, "School's out, so you have to spend the morning working with me before you go play." At first, I was offended that she was using our break time to make us work, but it did help me internalize at a young age that rhythms of work never stop. Part of our image-bearing nature is to see that there are always gardens to mulch, closets to organize, and meals to plan. Even on Saturdays and summers, this never-ending background work of ordering creation is precisely how we come to enjoy the summer evening when we finally rest. Understanding that there is always more work we could do is also what makes the sabbath break so radical—a topic we will come to momentarily.

Teaching Them the Fun Inherent in Communal Work

I'll never forget one night when I told the boys to clean the living room and their response wasn't, "Do we have to?" but rather, "Can we do the pick-up where we throw all the toys again?" A couple of nights before, we had made a game of it, where I held up the toy baskets and they tried to make basketball shots with all the Matchbox cars that littered the floor. Even for us adults, this is in no small part what makes work tolerable—other people who know how to make work fun. We can start this early. Sometimes you put on music and dance while you sweep the floor. Sometimes you stop raking leaves to jump in the pile. Whatever it is, we can usually find some way to act out the truth of reality—play and work need not be so far apart.

Teaching Them What Words Can't

At the end of the day, there are some things we can't learn from our heads; we have to learn them from our hands. There is a soul-deep longing for the usefulness of work, and we can teach that to children only by putting them to work. As we do that, we can trust the good order that God made when he created us. This is about teaching work ethic, yes, but it is also so much more. The mental and spiritual reward of work is so significant because we were made for good work, body and soul. We go to and from work and rest and to and from work and play because we were made for that rhythm. Practicing these rhythms is a way to "taste and see" that the way God made us is good.[1]

Yes, this is quite hard. It is always a sacrifice for us to teach them how to do a task that we could do more easily ourselves, but the reward is theirs. Our sacrifice for their reward—here again, we see one of the central paradigms of parenting played out, just by asking them to sweep the floor.

3. Practicing Habits of Letting Children See the Work outside the Household

I still have this incredible memory as a child. My dad would be dropping us off at school and he would pull into the parking lot, then suddenly he would accelerate and swing back out of the parking lot. We'd all begin to cheer as he announced, "You're coming to work with me today." It wouldn't happen often, but when it did, it was such a special thing to come see my parent at work.

At the time, my dad was a lawyer and a state senator, and I would have had little to no understanding of what he did with his days—until I got invited into the office. I still did not understand much, of course, but I began to see that he read papers at his desk, he wrote notes to people, he talked on the phone a lot. All kinds of people who were really different from us would come sit on his couch, and he would make them laugh and feel comfortable. They would always seem so thankful when they left. I began to form an inarticulable impression that my dad *did* something for people, that they liked him for it, and that he seemed to enjoy his work as much as he seemed to enjoy anything in life. Almost as if he was made to serve others and found himself happy when he was doing it.

---

1. Ps. 34:8.

Did you hear that? That echo of the gospel at work? That we are created to love our neighbors, that almost certainly the primary way we love our neighbors is through our daily work, whether in the house or outside of the house? Try catechizing your kid to say, "Work is good, it is from God and for others, and we feel his pleasure when we work." That's wonderful, and as you read earlier, I'm all for catechisms, but those words are hieroglyphs on the page of the mind until they see you work and, moreover, see you enjoy it.

Of course, my dad's white-collar work was incredibly different than so many of the jobs we have in the world. His dad (my "Papa," as we called him) worked himself out of Great Depression poverty by his faithful daily labor in the shipyard, and I will also never forget the way my dad always made a point to honor jobs the world might not otherwise honor. I got to see my dad talk with US senators and gas station clerks, with millionaires and short-order cooks, but I never noticed a difference in how he treated them. Once, when a group of men came to repave our driveway, I remember him putting his hand on my shoulder and saying, "You see this? This is really good work. None of us knows how to make a driveway, but these guys do it so well. Don't you ever look down on people who work with their hands, and don't you ever be ashamed if that's what you do for work." My dad regularly helped me see work outside the house for the good work that God made it to be.

That's now why I love letting my kids come to my office and press the elevator buttons. Sure, they mess up all the dry-erase boards, inevitably knock over a stack of papers, and often end up under the desk watching an iPad while I try to tune out the noise and make a call or write a stock purchase agreement or an LLC operating agreement. But there is something uniquely special to letting them see me at work.

If you asked me why I think my work is good for the world, I would talk about the importance of business law and how we help de-risk economic transactions, which is key to economic stability, growth, innovation, and entrepreneurship. I'd talk about how these are all building blocks of shalom in the world. And I know my kids don't get any of that—yet. But they do get to see that I get paid to negotiate with people, to pick the right words and get them down on paper. At least they can envision the space in which I do that and see that I love it—even when it's hard and it makes me come home late.

And I try to carry on my dad's work of showing off other people's work too. Every time I pass a mall, I quiz my kids: What was my first job? "Coffee shop!" They know. Every time we pass a construction site, I remind them that I worked heavy landscaping in college and got to drive small bulldozers. (As you might imagine, they are much more impressed with this than with lawyering.) And even now I try to explain to them in passing comments at the dinner table what I do: "I was helping a doctor today figure out how to sell his doctor's office to a new owner," or, "I was writing a chapter in my book today."

Showcasing work like this is a bit like showing off the world God made. They don't have to understand it all yet, but someday the language and the practice will come together and they will see that work may be cursed—but it is still good. And it's not something to run from but something to run to.

The Pleasure of Working beside Someone Who Loves Us

When Ash was five, Lauren and I bought a new shelf to go inside the back door for the steadily multiplying number of backpacks and coats. It was a fairly simple Ikea-like assembly, but since the boys are absolutely fascinated by the power drill, I asked Ash if he wanted to stay up a bit past bedtime and pull the trigger on the drill for me.

You should've seen his face. I think it was the best part of his year. It took me roughly six times longer than if I would've done it alone, and he also dented one of the poles. But I didn't invite him to work with me because I needed the help. I invited him to help because I love him. If the main goal of work was efficiency, we would never invite kids into work. Their help is almost guaranteed to hurt. But what if the goal of work is not to get it done as fast as possible? What if work is far more spiritual than that? What if work is more about making us like God? What if it's about service? What if it's about, like Ash felt with the drill and I felt in the garage, the pleasure of working beside the one who loves us?

Work is the gift that God gives us, and we pass that gift on to our kids by inviting them into God's good world of work.

HABITS OF WORK
FORMING FAMILIES

Main Idea

We were created by God for good work. Parents should think carefully about how they can teach children the spiritual dignity of work and showcase all the good work there is to be done, inside and outside of the household.

Habits for Inviting Children into the Work of the Household

Things to try:

- Talk about the housework in a way that dignifies the work that is done there.
- If a child can do it for themselves, try your best not to do it for them.
- Teach them tasks as early as possible, whether picking up toys, hammering a nail, taking out trash, washing a dish, folding towels, wiping tables, or sweeping floors. Children remember these moments as bonding moments, even when they are work.
- Let them help host by greeting guests at the door and offering drinks or snacks, and then helping with clean-up after.
- Let them help you (even when it slows you down)— this may require adding margin in your life so that your housework is not always about maximizing efficiency.
- Work toward an age-appropriate chore system. Let them tangibly check things off and earn rewards, whether money or stickers or something else.

Key Image

We were made to work alongside God. This means we love working with people we love. You can parent in this truth by creating ways your children can work alongside you.

Showcasing Work

For any work that is outside of the home, consider whether it's possible to bring your kids with you sometime. If you work on a computer inside the home, consider taking time occasionally to let them see what you're doing and explain it.

> *"Work is not just a way to make the ends of life meet, work is better understood as an end that makes meaning of life."*

Talking about Work with Dignity

Explaining why we work is hard. Be ready to answer.

"WHY DO YOU HAVE TO GO TO WORK TODAY?"

"I *get* to go to work— which I'm actually really thankful for. Because God made us all to work. Some people don't have a job they like, and some don't have a job at all. Work is a blessing."

"WHAT DO YOU DO AT WORK?"

- "Just like God helps people, at work I get to help people by . . ."
- "Just like God created the world, at work I get to create things, like . . ."
- "Just like the Bible tells us to serve other people, at work I get to serve other people by . . ."

"WHY DO WE HAVE TO DO CHORES?"

"Just like God organized the world and made it a good place for us to live, it's our job to keep our house organized so it's a good place for us to live."

IN UNEMPLOYMENT, WE MIGHT SAY:

"God made us to work, so one of the reasons Mom/Dad is so sad right now is that they don't have a job to go to. It's sad like being really good at riding bikes, but not having one to enjoy it."

IN UNDEREMPLOYMENT, WE MIGHT SAY:

"God made us with special talents and tells us to use them, so one of the reasons Mom/Dad is so sad right now is that their job doesn't use their talents."

IN HARD TIMES OF OVERWORK, WE MIGHT SAY:

"Just like God works and then rests, one of the reasons it is so hard for Mom/Dad right now is that their job is not letting them rest, and good rest is just as important as good work."

Remember, you don't have to try everything at once. One small change can have big spiritual impact. Pick one thing to start.

Further Resources

Every Good Endeavor: Connecting Your Work to God's Work, Timothy Keller with Katherine Leary Alsdorf
The Gospel at Work: How Working for King Jesus Gives Purpose and Meaning to Our Jobs, Sebastian Traeger and Greg Gilbert
Kingdom Calling: Vocational Stewardship for the Common Good, Amy L. Sherman
Designing Your Life: How to Build a Well-Lived, Joyful Life, Bill Burnett and Dave Evans

A Note on Adapting

A lot of teaching kids about work depends on the work you do. Whether you're a stay-at-home parent or something else, take the time to think about how your work fits into the story of God. What part of creation does your job care for? In what ways is your job broken? In what ways could your job be redeemed? Understanding our own work is the first step to teaching our children about it.

A Workday Prayer, Adapted from John Calvin's Daily Prayers

My good God, Father, and Savior, grant me aid by your Holy Spirit to now work fruitfully in my vocation, which is from you, all in order to love you and the people around me rather than for my own gain and glory. Give me wisdom, judgment, and prudence, and freedom from my besetting sins. Bring me under the rule of true humility. Let me accept with patience whatever amount of fruitfulness or difficulty in my work that you give me this day. And in all I do, help me to rest always in my Lord Jesus Christ and in his grace alone for my salvation and life. Hear me, merciful Father, by our Lord Jesus Christ, Amen.

> **We Always Need the Reminder of Grace:** God's love inspires our action, but our action does not inspire God's love. Our family habits will not change God's love for us, but God's love for us should change our family habits.

CHAPTER 8

PLAY

"Pretend you're a steamroller!" Coulter shouts as we roll around on the bedroom floor. "No! Pretend you're a bulldog!" Ash chimes in. "Yeah, bulldog!" Coulter agrees. I begin romping around and chasing them on all fours. They squeal with glee and try to escape.

For years and years now, I have heard two commands over and over from my children, and they are related: "Play with me" and "Pretend." We just talked about the innate need to work, but have you ever thought about the innate need to play? Why is it that children seem built to play and pretend?

It is because in the story of God, we were made for another world—a world of unfettered joy.

Play as Imagining the Kingdom

A Christian is no ordinary observer of the world. Our faith asks us to believe that angels and demons exist, that a virgin gave birth, that a man named Jesus rose from the dead, and that a new kingdom is coming where we all get to celebrate and play, happily ever after. Our faith asks us to believe that things are not the way they seem, and that despite what we experience, suffering and evil will not have the final word. This is not easy. In Christianity, you won't get very far without a healthy imagination.

That's not because this story of God is all made up but rather because it is so real; the world is so much more than meets the eye. This is the wisdom of all fairy tales and of any good kids' movie—that things are more than they seem. Extraordinary things are patiently waiting, right here in this reality, to be discovered.

This is a core truth of the biblical story, and one that children are especially suited to sniff out. This is why, perhaps, Jesus tells us that unless we become like children, we won't enter the kingdom of heaven. Children are the ones humble enough to believe that there is far more to reality than there seems.

This playful Christian imagination does not diminish the reality of evil, though it does help us understand a parent's role in that reality. I often think about the tragically wonderful movie *Life Is Beautiful*, in which a father convinces his son that their imprisonment in a concentration camp is a complicated game. In doing so, he protects the innocence of his child's joy, even as the horrors of evil surround them. Creating laughter in a death camp—it is one of the most haunting and inspiring takes on the role of a parent. In some way, we are the guardians, holding back the onslaught of all the world's darkness, so that the living room can become a place of imagination and play.

Play is thus a way to reenchant a disenchanted world.[1] This

---

1. Part of my background for the idea of Christian habits reenchanting a disenchanted world is Charles Taylor's argument that a key feature of our "secular age" is living within a world that cannot see beyond the material. For more on this, see his work *A Secular Age* (Cambridge, MA: Belknap, 2007), or James K. A. Smith's helpful primer *How (Not) to Be Secular: Reading Charles Taylor* (Grand Rapids, MI: Eerdmans, 2014). Mike Cosper also expounds on these themes in *Recapturing the Wonder: Transcendent Faith in a Disenchanted World* (Downers Grove, IL: InterVarsity Press,

is serious business. Think about it. A world without play is a world without magic. And a world without magic is a world without resurrection. And in a world without resurrection, nothing good can come true. Which means every fairy tale is a lie. Play, then, is a rebellion against the greatest lie. It is an act of war in allegiance to the greatest truth—that Christ is risen and fairy tales really do come true—namely, the one we're living in. Hallelujah! Let's pause the tasks, then, and play ourselves into Easter people.

So it is that to play—I mean to really play—is an exercise of imagining the kingdom, a practice of bearing witness to it right in our own living rooms and back yards.

Habits of play must then be a practice of the Christian household because they echo the kingdom to come. There are infinite ways to do this, but I suggest three as easy places to begin:

1. Habitually read imaginative stories to them.
2. Habitually accept their invitations to play.
3. Habitually send them out to play on their own.

1. Habitually Read Imaginative Stories to Them

We are all born with this longing for another world, but it is not a given that we will keep it. Our fallen world has a way of dulling our imaginations and training us to accept much less than the glory of the kingdom that God is building through Jesus and his church. For that reason, we have to see that training and exercising the imagination are as righteous as training and exercising

---

2017). The common theme is how all of our cultural assumptions run against the reality of the divine, which means our default cultural mood actively dims our spiritual imagination. In such a moment, what better inheritance can we give our children than a pattern of habits that helps them be aware from a young age that the world is enchanted with the presence of God?

the body or the mind. The primary means of this exercise is story. Especially imaginative stories.

One of the things I love about Lauren is that she is a voracious reader, and she loves offering the gift of good books to our children. There is a daily checklist on our refrigerator where she marks whether each child has been read to, or, for the older ones, whether they have spent time reading. And while this is of course important for education and development of thought, I want to focus on the oft-overlooked glory of stories—their spiritual capacity to enlarge our imagination.

Without a Christian imagination, what would we do with verses about mountains breaking into song and trees clapping?[2] How can we imagine captives being set free[3] or a rescuer of the world riding in on a white horse?[4] We need big imaginations to be able to handle the big visions of the Bible, lest they mean nothing to us. When we engage with literature—for example, by reading the famous modern fantasy stories of our time, like Harry Potter, The Lord of the Rings, or The Chronicles of Narnia—we exercise this capacity.[5] Never mind that these things aren't "real." The more important fact is that they are true. They echo the biblical story of sacrificial love, courage, overcoming evil, and death as the ultimate enemy. A capacity for fiction is as important as a knowledge of history.

When I tell my kids stories about Pet Blue, a secret, blue pet dragon that my brother and I had when we were little, the

---

2. Isa. 55:12.
3. Luke 4:18.
4. Rev. 19:11.
5. See Sarah Mackenzie, *The Read-Aloud Family: Making Meaningful and Lasting Connections with Your Kids* (Grand Rapids, MI: Zondervan, 2018) and the related website https://readaloudrevival.com. Of course, this is true of imaginative movies too, though part of the power of written stories is that they ask more of our imaginations. When there are no pictures to do the work for us, we have to imagine the ship or the princess or the battle, and that is good spiritual and neurological work.

little ones get immediately engrossed in the story. They sit down wide-eyed, delighted by a pet dragon that protects kids and fights robbers. At some point they inevitably ask, "But is Pet Blue real? Did you really have a dragon?" When they are old enough, I say, "It's a story, but even stories have real power." And they get it. This is training for real life, because often there is more truth in good fiction and poetry than in the news.[6] And our hearts need that. In hearing good stories, what we're doing is exercising our imaginations because believing in the truest story takes a sanctified imagination.

2. Habitually Accept Their Invitations to Play

My friend Steve always asks me if I've been baking bread. I love baking bread, but I can do it only when my work is calm enough and life is in order enough for me to have a blank Saturday morning to pay attention to the slow rise of a loaf. So it doesn't happen often, but that's why he asks; baking bread is a sign that my life is in order. If it has been months since I've done it, it is probably because I'm letting myself get too busy.

I think regular play with children is a similar sign that something in the household is going right. Because it can easily feel like there is always something better to do. My kids ask me fifty times a day to play with them—and that's only a fraction of the requests Lauren gets. Of course, there's always something that seems more urgent—I've got clients waiting on emails and payroll needs to be run. There's a patch of drywall that needs to be replaced. I have a talk to prepare or a draft chapter to work on. The list is never ending—that's true for all of us, which is

---

6. William Carlos Williams, "Asphodel, That Greeny Flower," *Journey to Love* (New York: Random House, 1955): "It is difficult / to get the news from poems, / yet men die miserably every day / for lack / of what is found there."

why we need rhythms of play with children to interrupt all this serious stuff and remind us that the world doesn't depend on it.

Think about what it means to play with children. It means leaving this world and entering another one. It means becoming Lucy and stepping into a wardrobe only to find that the back of it leads to another world.[7] This is a world where dolls talk and LEGOs fly. This is a world where robbers are coming from the attic and broomsticks are horses to ride away on. Like imaginative reading, the capacity to get lost in play is practice for the kingdom for both parent and child.

Let me note two concerns. First, as you are aware, you are reading the writings of a father. Specifically, one who is out of the house between breakfast and dinner. This means I need habits to really engage with my kids when I am there so they get all of me. For a stay-at-home parent, the more important habit here is going to be making sure there is some small space for giving full, undistracted attention to children (maybe half an hour before a nap, or the hour after breakfast), but mostly, a stay-at-home parent is going to be focused on the next habit, of sending them out to play. Because you cannot, and should not, spend all of your time playing with your children. They don't need that from us. But what they do need is our enthusiastic play in regular rhythms and, as we will discuss below, our firm commands to go play elsewhere in regular rhythms.

For me, every evening right after work is a time when the kids know my phone is getting turned off and we're doing what they want to do. Lauren usually reserves half an hour in the morning when tasks get set aside and she can say yes to play or reading to them. Saturday mornings are also boys' mornings,

---

7. C. S. Lewis, *The Lion, the Witch, and the Wardrobe: A Story for Children* (New York: HarperCollins, 1950).

where Lauren reliably gets to sleep in and the boys and I go find an adventure. These times will vary for all families, but the point is developing your own expected rhythms where you find play and shared activities together.

Second, as kids get older, this will look much less like imaginative play and more like cultivating enchantment with the world. What I mean is that as we mature, our play will look different, but we ought not lose the wonder that God's creation is magnificent and full of possibility. For older children and teens, this will mean helping them cultivate space and awe for hobbies and activities that bring joy.

In both cases, and no matter what their age, habits of regularly playing or engaging with our kids necessarily means that we do hard things like focus. Like turn our phones off. Like go outside, rain or shine. Like get on the ground and get dirty and make our backs hurt. Like make time for trips and outings. Like run around and get sweaty. Little takes more work than playing with children, which means we can't do it all the time. But we can have expected rhythms of it.

3. Habitually Send Them Out to Play on Their Own

Again, no parent can, or should, always accept their children's invitations to play. And we shouldn't feel guilty about that. On the contrary, we should recognize that when we say no to play and send them out on their own, something important is happening. Whether this is sending kids to the back yard or telling your teen to turn off the TV and go take a hike, instructing them to go out and engage with the world on their own means we invite them to get comfortable with the struggle against boredom (which is really just the struggle against the fallen imagination) and do the good work of play by themselves.

As our children get older, this should look more like creating space for them to engage the world, rather than simply sending them out to play. But this is equally, if not more, important.

It is entirely possible to unconsciously indoctrinate our children into our broken view of the world, that life is fundamentally about what we can accomplish and there isn't time for much else. This may be in the academics we push them to or in the sports schedules we try to keep. But if we find that life is too busy for them to have downtime to engage with the world, then something is wrong.

One of the claims of this book is that Christian families cannot default to the American rule of life—we must fight for better habits. One of the places this is most urgent is helping our kids not engage in a life that is so busy that they don't have space for imaginative reading, long conversations with friends, silent reflection, hobbies that are just for fun (not for getting into college), a walk in nature, a road trip with friends, a church retreat—the list goes on. We know that we were created by God to work, but there is so much more to life than work—there is play and rest too.

One of the paramount ways we can model this balance is by balancing our family rhythms of work and play with a sabbath rhythm.

Practicing the Habit of Sabbath

The idea that families should be sabbathing as a household habit may make as much sense in a chapter on work as in a chapter on play, but I place it here to try to emphasize one of the unique features of sabbath—there is something playful about the command to rest. It is certainly enchanting. Sabbath is a whimsical rebellion against the idea that work is the only important thing in the world. Sabbath looks at the tired, overworked American and smiles with compassion, inviting us into a rhythm of renewal that we desperately need.

Sabbath is a practical habit with no end of theological significance. Just as play is an exercise in looking forward to the kingdom to come, sabbath is an exercise in remembering our salvation. Sabbath rest is a firm reminder that the real work of the world has been finished in Jesus' death on the cross.[8] We have much that God has called us to do, but we don't have anything to prove. When we develop family rhythms of rest, we model the truth of our salvation in real life—we can rest, because God has done his good work.

For our family, sabbathing includes the obvious rest from the week's work—but it is much more than that too. It is not enough to stop the nine-to-five and pause the laundry, we also try to start the play and the rest. With young children, we try to light a candle sometime on Saturday evening to mark the beginning of our sabbath. The communal play begins then. It may be an outing for the kids, and later it likely means a night when Lauren or I go to see friends for conversation, invite someone over, or maybe have a night when we just stay home and enjoy something together that doesn't involve cleaning or emails.

On Sunday, our rest from work is held up by twin pillars of worship and community.

The first thing to define the day is corporate worship. This is not just podcasting a sermon, this is participating in the embodied rhythm of a local church. There are whole books to be written here about habits of the household and the rhythms of the local church, but that is not my focus. This book is mostly focused on the habits inside the household. Nonetheless, it should be clearly noted that the rhythms of our household must be in

---

8. John 19:30: "It is finished."

sync with the rhythms of the household of God as embodied in the local church.

The second pillar of sabbath for us is a communal gathering. I know friends who practice this with extended family, like we do, and friends who practice it with other friends. But part of our sabbath rest as parents means getting together with my extended family, sharing a meal, and letting the cousins all play together. This is chaotic, to be sure (there are six of us brothers and sisters, and fifteen and counting kids between us all), but it is equally restful to have all the other parents around to help share the work and to find the rest of good food and conversation with a family that feels like friends.

By Sunday evening, when we come home, we are starting the work of the week again by getting ready for Monday. In the best of ways, we are tired out from the playful work of rest, while at the same time rested up for the coming week of work.

These are holy rhythms, and they keep life in step with the story of God.

Implicit Memory and Rhythms of Play

In the story of God, our children were made for good work, good play, and good rest, which means we need habits to form them in who they were meant to be.

Child psychologists write about something called implicit memory. It's the part of you that remembers things without being aware that you are remembering them. For example, it is one thing to walk into a room and consciously recall, "This is where my mom and I had that awful fight," or "This is where my dad always came home from work angry." That's explicit memory. It is another thing to see your old house and simply feel scared or stressed because memory association is telling you that this was a place where you were not safe or happy. That's implicit memory.

It is by implicit memory that we feel our way into the future. We imagine the future in versions of the past. This is why implicit memory is the tragedy and the glory of childhood.

Picture rhythms of work and play and rest as one of the ways we can give our children a rich inheritance of positive implicit memory.

When we talk about work and involve them in it as part of God's good creation, and when we regularly lose it in the silliness and laughter of play, and when we regularly rest as a family endeavor, we weave them a fabric of memory that befits the kingdom God is bringing. We help them imagine the future in ways it should be. That is planting a seed of the kingdom in their childhood. And God is faithful to grow it.

HABITS OF PLAY

FORMING FAMILIES

Main Idea

Getting lost in fun and imaginative play is an echo of the kingdom to come, a sign of a world that is full of joy. Practicing good habits of play is a way of cultivating a more Christian imagination that foreshadows the kingdom to come.

Lauren's Starter List for Reading

Lauren is the great curator of good reads in our family. Here are her top five in a few categories to pass on the love of reading. You can find more of Lauren's Lists on https:// www.habitsofthehousehold.com/laurenslists.

Five Great Books to Read to Little Ones

- *Where the Wild Things Are* by Maurice Sendak
- *Owl Moon* by Janet Yolen
- *Never Ask a Dinosaur to Dinner* by Gareth Edwards and Guy Parker-Rees
- *The Snowy Day* by Ezra Jack Keats
- *The Little Mouse, the Red Ripe Strawberry, and the Big Hungry Bear* by Don and Audrey Wood

Five Great Book Series to Read Aloud to Kids Five and Over

- The Wingfeather Saga by Andrew Peterson
- The Chronicles of Narnia by C. S. Lewis
- The Green Ember series by S. D. Smith
- Little House series by Laura Ingalls Wilder
- Redwall series by Brian Jacques

Five Great Imaginative Stories for Older Readers

- *A Wrinkle in Time* by Madeleine L'Engle
- Harry Potter series by J. K. Rowling
- The Dark Is Rising series by Susan Cooper
- *The Adventures of Tom Sawyer* by Mark Twain
- The Lord of the Rings trilogy by J. R. R. Tolkien

Note: Don't stop reading aloud once they can read! Reading is a wonderful way to bond the family together. This includes audio books and reading to each other.

> *"In Christianity, you won't get very far without a healthy imagination."*

Habits for Cultivating Moments of Play

Things to try:

- If you're a parent who is out of the house each day, think about making half an hour before or after a concentrated time for presence.
- If you're a parent who is with the kids all day, don't feel guilty about not playing with them constantly. That's not best for either of you. But remember that ten focused minutes of engagement or attention each day could go a long way.
- Draw clear distinctions between when you are playing with them and when they need to play alone or with other kids.
- When you decide to play, treat it like work—stay focused and present. Don't bring devices.

Ideas for Structuring a Family Sabbath

Things to discuss:

- When do you start? Could you mark the moment?
- What's one thing to stop during sabbath?
- What's one thing to lean into during sabbath?
- How is worship included?
- Should the outdoors be included?
- What's one family activity that is restful for everyone?
- Could you join forces with friends or family?
- Do you need to limit devices on the sabbath?

Further Resources

ON READING

The Read-Aloud Family: Making Meaningful and Lasting Connections with Your Kids, Sarah Mackenzie (see also the website https://readaloudrevival.com)
100 Best Books for Children, Anita Silvey

ON REENCHANTING THE WORLD

Telling the Truth: The Gospel as Tragedy, Comedy, and Fairy Tale, Frederick Buechner
Recapturing the Wonder: Transcendent Faith in a Disenchanted World, Mike Cosper

ON SABBATH

Liturgy of the Ordinary: Sacred Practices in Everyday Life, Tish Harrison Warren

A Note on Adapting

At its core, play is the idea that we engage with the world in wonder. This is not limited by age, size, or health. Think about how you can help cultivate an enchantment with the world God made, wherever you are.

We Always Need the Reminder of Grace: God's love inspires our action, but our action does not inspire God's love. Our family habits will not change God's love for us, but God's love for us should change our family habits.

CHAPTER 9

———

CONVERSATION

O n a Saturday at 7 p.m., most of the boys are in their pajamas, but they are scuttling around the back yard with large, sharp tools. This is because some friends are coming over for a backyard fire, and they are "helping" me start the fire by making the process twice as long and three times as dangerous.

It's usually quite a spectacle, as it involves them collecting sticks from our substantial brush pile behind the back fence, dragging out every sharp tool from the basement, putting said tools to work in some way they are not meant to be used, and also using up a whole box of matches. Usually I'm managing chaos, teetering on the thin border between good fun to irresponsibility: "Don't saw that close to your hand." "You cannot swing a hatchet if your brother's behind you." "No, we're not going to use gasoline this time."

But besides the natural itch that gets scratched by breaking things and lighting things on fire, the reason I value letting them into the process is that it is a way to let them see the trappings of conversation and friendship.

Recently, Whit got the privilege of not just helping start the fire but hanging around for the first hour of it. We sat in camp chairs together, and as guys began to trickle in the back fence, he watched the rituals of friendship: A clap of the hands and a hug. A nod and a nickname. Grabbing something from the cooler and finding a chair. The jibes and the jokes he doesn't understand but laughs at anyway. And eventually, the settling into conversation as the twilight dims and the fire takes over.

I think of this as a sacred invitation because I think of conversation as a sacred ritual. It is the rhythm of the household that turns family into friends, and friends into family. Conversation—inside and outside of the household—is the learned art of friendship. But you cannot learn the art without practice, and that takes the habit of finding rhythms of one-on-one conversation.

Conversation in the Story of God

I imagine a similar ritual playing out toward the end of a day in Eden. The sun begins to cool, and someone is setting up a chair under the tree on a hill for a good look at the sky, waiting for the horizon to trade the sun for the stars. I imagine them fussing over getting a bowl of fruit or nuts ready, mumbling, "He'll be coming by any minute now."

We can only imagine what these conversations with God were like in Eden because the first glimpse we get of them happens *after* Adam and Eve ate the forbidden fruit. When God comes walking in the garden at the cool of the day, Adam and Eve hide because, of course, they have sinned. They hide because they have broken relationship.

The pain lingering in these verses is monolithic. Genesis seems to suggest that Adam and Eve are skipping out on the evening ritual, that God is taking his evening walk and looking for his people, his creatures, his friends, to join him as they often do. But they are not home. They are hiding from conversation.

To sit and talk with God is the pinnacle of human existence. And yet still Adam and Eve (and we) hide from this essential connection. That is the tragedy. But the story of Scripture is how he comes to find us out. He pursues the one-on-one with us anyway. That is the love story.

I believe there is a fundamental similarity between prayer with God and conversation with friends because in each, we are reaching toward the divine paradigm we were made for—to commune in conversation, to know and be known through words and presence. To sense a shared ownership of each other.

As the Bible says in Revelation, "They will be his people, and God himself will be with them and be their God."[1] In the final communion, we are fully present with God—not as individuals but as a people, because we are also fully present to each other.

Friendship across Generations

I will never forget a conversation I had with my mom and dad the week before Lauren and I got married. My parents took Lauren and me out to dinner at a nice restaurant to celebrate the upcoming wedding. At the time, we were both twenty-two.

I remember about halfway through the meal feeling a tremendous sense of happiness—but I had no idea why. Was it because I was getting married? Because I got to order a nice steak and didn't have to pay? Because Lauren seemed happy?

It didn't dawn on me until after the main course, when my dad ordered drinks for everyone so we could sit longer and sip and talk. I was happy because I had an evening to linger in conversation with my mom and dad, not just as a child but as their friend.

---

1. Rev. 21:3.

As I listened to my parents' advice on marriage, as I asked them questions about their marriage, as I watched them engage the girl I loved in conversation, I felt known by them. I felt the peculiar pleasure of friendship with my parents.

I might venture to say that this moment, repeated over and over in different ways, is the ultimate goal of family: to make friends of each other.

And the consummation of friendship, of course, is conversation.

We practice conversation in the household to teach the spiritual art of friendship, that we might befriend each other, and train our children to go out and befriend the world. Here are three practical habits I have found help this sacred effort:

1. Pursue one-on-one moments.
2. Practice conversation as a way to heal trauma.
3. Model vulnerability.

1. Pursue One-on-One Moments

Each birthday, I do two things with my sons. First, I write them a letter. They don't get to read it. For the most part, they don't even know about it. It's not a letter to them now, it is a letter to their future selves. I suppose I'll give them a box of them when they are eighteen and leave the house, or sixteen, if we're having a rough year—who knows. The reason I love doing this is because it gives me a regular opportunity to write to them like friends.

In writing a letter to their older selves, I don't hesitate to use bigger words, share my own fears and advice, or describe what Lauren and I were going through when they were five and didn't know that parents "went through" anything. I tell them about who they are and about who I am, and I wonder aloud about who I see us all becoming.

In the letters, I talk to them like a friend. Because at the end of things, that's what I hope we become.

The second thing that I do on their birthdays is I take them out to breakfast—with just me. Part of this is to create a special moment of pancakes and waffles. But really, it is to give them the gift of being pursued in conversation. I always bring a journal and a list of questions. At a young age, I ask them things like, What is your favorite food? What is your favorite game? What is your favorite story Mama reads you? What's your best wrestling move? Favorite animal? It's almost all silly and descriptive, and yet, as I jot down the answers and look back at them, I see in their eyes the pleasure I felt at the dinner table with my parents, the honor of being pursued in conversation.

As some of the kids have gotten older, the questions are more nuanced and run deeper: What do you love doing? What's hard about life right now? Who is your best friend? What do you think you're good at? What do you want to get better at? When do you feel nervous? What's your favorite book? What do you find yourself praying about often? What do you think about when you lie in bed? What do you wish you were allowed to do that you're not?

By itself, a pancake breakfast with a couple of questions is a nice morning, a quaint idea, at best. But that's the practical lens. When we look at it through the liturgical lens, this is not just a moment, it's the beginning of a rhythm that shapes us. As we look for other times and spaces throughout year, the art of one-on-one conversation becomes a habit.

Here are some of the times and spaces we look for.

The Car

I mentioned earlier that one of the reasons we don't do screens in the car as a normal rhythm is that the car is such a conducive place for conversation. In the car we have the advantage of both looking out the window at a "third thing," which is often the posture of good conversation. Even more, in the car you are in the in-between. You are coming from something or going to something, and it is often in the in-between moments that our brains and hearts process what is happening in life. When everyone is in the car, especially at young ages, this is more likely to be chaos. But when it is only one or two in the car, those should be signal moments to be open to possible conversation.

Early Mornings and Late Evenings

Someone always has to be the first one up and the last one to bed. I often find that these spaces afford moments with one of my sons to engage them in a way that they won't engage when others are around. These spaces nearest to sleep seem like thin spaces. Sometimes we're just tired, but other times we are uniquely available. If I sense that, I will ask a question.

Third Things

As with the car, so much of our life of conversation happens when we have a third thing that brings us together. That is to say, there are two people and then a third thing that mediates the interaction between the two. There may be something Trinitarian here, but I'll keep it practical. Plucking guitars or raking leaves, baking bread or stoking a fire, fishing, knitting, hiking, stargazing, sweeping floors, or even running errands—there are all sorts of activities that are wonderful because they keep two people in the same place and are mindless enough to allow us to engage each other in real conversation. Find these things, pick ones your kids like, and use them to find each other in conversation.

Special Outings

I think part of the reason my moment at dinner with my parents was so special was because there were six kids in my family and it was very rare to get a one-on-one moment with them as a child. This is an unavoidable truth: the bigger (and busier) a family gets, the harder it is to have naturally occurring one-on-one moments. But while it might be an uphill journey to find these times, it is a climb worth taking. Our children need those moments. One of the ways we do this is if Lauren has to run an errand on a Saturday and the rest of us are staying home, sometimes she'll take the gift of alone time, or once in a while she will invite a boy to come along so they might have space and time in the car talking. Another way is simply occasionally taking the opportunity to do a one-on-one outing just for the heck of it. A couple of months ago I took only Ash out on a bike ride along the James River trails, just on a whim. Halfway through our ride, as we sat by the water eating beef jerky, he suddenly began telling me everything he'd ever thought of. All six-year-old thoughts, but I had never heard him say so many things. He is often the quieter one, but he just kept going. Something about a one-on-one outing with a parent can unlock the sense that they are special, loved, and worth discovering, and so they talk. This is exactly what we are looking for in a special outing.

2. Practice Conversation as a Way to Heal Trauma

One Saturday, I was playing the guitar upstairs when I heard Ash yell from the back door, "Papa, come quick! Coulter is hurt real bad." I knew instantly that his voice was different, and I bounded down the stairs, almost knocking Ash and his cousin Abe over at the bottom.

I found Coulter in the back yard, leaning over a swing, holding his arm and moaning. His arm was dripping with blood.

As I swept him up, I covered his eyes so I could look at his arm without his seeing the wound. When I saw it, I knew two things immediately: he would need some serious stitches, but he was going to be okay.

Skin heals rather quickly—that was a given for him at his age—but what was not a given was whether his mind would heal. I could see him standing there dazed and scared—traumatized. He was only three, but he had somehow gotten his arm caught while swinging on the rope swing. He was standing alone in the back yard bleeding. People were coming out the door yelling. I was taking my shirt off and wrapping his arm and then running him to the car.

This was an emergency moment, and I knew that his young brain was doing all kinds of shifts and creating new pathways— structures he would hold for a long time and that would affect him in deep ways.[2] While I could trust the doctors to stitch the skin back together, I knew it was up to us—his parents—to use words to stitch the mind back together.

So as I carried him to the car, I looked at him and smiled, saying, "You're going to be okay, Coulter." He had the look of shock and seemed confused. "We're going to go to the doctors. They are going to be really nice to you and help you. They're going to make it stop hurting, and then I'm going to be so proud of you and we are going to get a special treat." He didn't respond much, but he perked up when he heard "treat."

The rest of the afternoon and evening went more or less like that. Throughout the day I retold Coulter the story of what had happened and retold the story of what would happen, and soon, he started to catch on.

---

2. I have found Adam Young's insights in his podcast *The Place We Find Ourselves* to be very helpful in understanding how these kinds of childhood moments, especially traumatic ones, shape us.

"What happened?" I would ask him.

"I was playing in the back yard and got my arm stuck." The first two times he told me this, just mentioning it made him burst into tears. And we would just stop there. But by the fourth or fifth time, he was processing it.

So I'd ask him, "And did your brother Ash run to get help right away?"

"Yes," he would answer.

"And did I run outside to help you right away?"

"Yeah."

"And did we rush to the doctors so they could help you?"

"Yeah."

"So all these people are all helping you?"

As we went through the journey of the day together, plot elements got added to the story.

"And what did we do in the waiting room?"

"We read books."

"And what did they give you for your stitches?"

"Lots of stickers!"

"And what did that doctor tell you?"

"That I was the bravest kid."

"And then what did we go buy?"

"Donuts!"

Standing on the porch that night with his brothers and cousins, Coulter told everyone the story of his stitches—but now, it was not a story of being hurt and alone with blood in the back yard but a story of family helping him, calling him brave, and celebrating with donuts. After that, it wasn't surprising to me that even with his bandaged arm, Coulter got back on the rope swing again the next day, and that he smiles when he talks about his stitches.

Through the work of conversation, the story of trauma had been made a story of triumph.

Conversation heals trauma. This is true for children in the back yard, teenagers in the difficulties of high school, and adults who carry their dark stories. Trauma—whether physical or emotional—affects us deeply, body and soul. Moments of trauma reorganize our patterns of thinking. Sometimes, these are the awful moments we typically associate with trauma. But it's important to know that traumatic moments can also happen at much more ordinary moments of hurt, loneliness, fear, or anger. It's important to remember that the most important role of a parent is not protecting them from these moments but identifying them and repairing them after they happen. This is where conversation comes in.

At worst, we can go years, or even our whole lives, living in the stunted patterns that fear or pain caused. Unless, of course, it is healed. And most often, the way we heal is through organized conversation.

Sometimes we call it counseling, sometimes therapy, sometimes having someone who listens, sometimes it's repentance and forgiveness—but in all cases, it comes through another human being who will look you in the eye and talk to you in the right way.

You cannot save your children from pain. Trauma will find them just like it has found us. But one of the great gifts of being a parent is that we teach them the healing power of conversation.

We can start simply by finding them in conversation and helping them talk through the pain that life inevitably brings.

3. Model Vulnerability

By the end of my first year in college, I knew my life was headed in a bad direction. I had spent my whole first year away from home rebelling against everything I was taught. But all the drinking and girls and secret evenings were not setting me free like I thought they would; they were a crushing weight on my back. I was not the kind of person I wanted to be. But I didn't know what to do.

That summer, my dad invited me on a trip with him. He had a conference in Toronto, and he brought me along for two nights. I remember at dinner in the hotel the first night, I so badly wanted to confess to my dad, and tell him what I had been up to, and how I was sorry, and how I wanted to change but didn't know how—but I couldn't figure out how to start.

I look back at that restaurant table as a picture of the human condition. We are so close to telling our secrets, so close to being found in conversation, but right on the edge of a moment that would change our lives, we get scared. Like Adam and Eve, we hide back in the bushes.

But that night my dad did something. Unprompted, he started telling me about struggles he had when he was younger. About the ways he wrestled with things he was conflicted about.

He was vulnerable. And suddenly, I felt the freedom to do the same. So I started talking.

That night changed my life. Without exaggeration. After confessing to my dad, seeking his forgiveness for some things and asking for advice and wisdom for other things, I returned from Toronto with a burden lifted. Conversation had changed everything, and I went back to school free from my weights and free to live differently. And I did. The last three years of college were totally different, and I began walking with the Lord in a way I never had.

One of the unique opportunities of a parent is to use conversation to walk your child through their mess. But vulnerability is not a given, and usually a child is honest because a parent is honest first. A child is vulnerable because a parent demonstrates it. A child engages in conversation because a parent seeks them out.

This is the great burden and blessing of parenting—we have the opportunity and the duty to seek out our children and use conversation to help heal the pain that we all carry.

Trauma and secrets can burn us up from the inside out,[3] but conversation is what turns those destructive fires of our own fallenness into the refining fire of God's grace. And so often it comes through the grace of conversation.

The School of Love as a School of Friendship

Go back with me to the moment where we started, with all of the kids helping me start the fire. Later on that night, after all of the boys eventually went to bed, my friends and I sat out late to talk. We talked about work and kids and church and politics. We got deep and shared things we were struggling with. We lightened up and made fun of each other. We retold stories we all know every word to but like hearing again anyway. In the end, by becoming a bit more of friends, we all came away a bit more human. A bit closer to each other, and a bit closer to God because of that.

We've been practicing this for years. The kind of friendships that make or break life do not happen by chance encounters one evening, and they are not a given—they happen over a lifetime of practice.

Habits of conversation are the beginning of that life, and we can give the gift of friendship by teaching those habits in the household.

---

3. Ps. 32:3: "When I kept silent, my bones wasted away . . ."

HABITS OF CONVERSATION

FORMING FAMILIES

Main Idea

Conversation is the rhythm that turns family into friends and friends into family. Teaching habits of conversation is the way we begin teaching habits of friendship.

Considering Times for Conversations

- Use a parenting check-in to keep in mind important conversations that may need to be had with a child.
- Potential conversation times:
  - » Car rides
  - » Yardwork/chores/house projects
  - » Family trips
  - » Around a fire
  - » Taking a child out for a special one-on-one meal/treat
  - » After bedtime

Creating Spaces for Conversations

- Do you have a room that kids and adults are comfortable sitting in?
- Is there a room without a TV?
- Are phones put away when at the table?
- Can you put chairs on a porch or in the yard?
- Could a family walk be a rhythm?
- Could you light a candle or a fire?

"Conversation—inside and outside of the household—is the learned art of friendship."

Some Starter Questions for Kid Conversations

About the Day:

- What was the best and worst part of today? Anything you laughed at?
- Did anyone get in trouble today?
- Does anyone in your class not have a friend?
- What did you think about before you fell asleep last night?
- Who do you like sitting by in class? Who do you not want to sit by?

About Life:

- What's your favorite thing to do with Mom/Dad/brother/sister/friend?
- Who is your best friend right now? Anyone you're mad at?
- What do you think you're really good at? Bad at?
- What is the bravest thing you've done?
- Is there anything you want to tell me or ask me about?
- Is there anything you notice about the world that you think other people don't notice?
- What do you pray about when you talk to God? When do you pray?

A Note on Friendship

Teaching conversation and friendship as a parent presumes you practice it. Make sure there is space in your life where you pursue vulnerability and adult conversation with friends.

Further Resources

Spiritual Friendship, Aelred of Rievaulx
The Common Rule: Habits of Purpose for an Age of Distraction, Justin Whitmel Earley (chapter on the weekly habit of conversation)

A Note on Adapting

As kids age, conversation becomes more possible, and far more important. We can't force children to talk, but we can create rhythms of being available and modeling vulnerability.

We Always Need the Reminder of Grace: God's love inspires our action, but our action does not inspire God's love. Our family habits will not change God's love for us, but God's love for us should change our family habits.

CHAPTER 10

BEDTIME

It was 1 a.m. when I woke to Shep crying. I trudged down the hall, trying to stay calm.

There are a number of reasons this was incredibly frustrating. He was a one-year-old at the time, and there was no reason he shouldn't have been sleeping through the night—but he still wasn't. That fall I had been traveling a lot, so I was getting to that place where I was not just physically tired, I was soul-tired. And to add insult to injury, I remember thinking that week that this would (finally) be the week I would catch up on sleep . . . but here I was.

I walked in his room, hoping just to pick him up, calm him, and put him back down. But when I picked him up, I immediately knew he was going to fight. His body went stiff, and he was trying to wiggle out of my hands.

Sixty seconds later, I found myself raising my voice in the middle of the night, saying, "No! Not now! No!" and trying to discipline a one-year-old who doesn't understand anything that is happening. As I heard myself barking, I realized the stupidity and futility of it, and I resigned. I put him down (not gently) and said, "Fine, just cry then." And I stormed back to my bed.

I laid down, momentarily hoping to indulge the fiction that

I could go back to sleep on that note, and as I did, I suddenly had the kind of clarity of thought that can come only with the conviction of the Holy Spirit, and I thought, "You're trying to use your anger to control him when you should be using your love to console him."

This concerned me. Because what I realized as I lay there in the bed was that this is not just something I did. This is something I often do. Put more bluntly, this is who I am. I am the kind of person who uses anger to control my family when I should use love to console and shepherd my family.

Keep in mind, this was years after my hallway realization that began this book. Here I am a couple of years later with one more child, and parenting is still really hard. Especially in the middle of the night.

I felt like a failure. But even worse, I felt like a failure on repeat. Despite all the work I had done in the meantime on parenting habits and liturgies, I was still an angry and impatient person.

These moments are important to lean into because in the story of God, coming to the end of ourselves isn't a sign of failure, it's the beginning of grace.

Failure and Grace in the Story of God

In a very real sense, parenting is one long process of revealing who you are. And usually that is not pretty.

Perhaps it's a one-year-old who won't sleep. Or maybe it's a pre-teen who talks back constantly, a five-year-old who is still wetting the bed, a third-grader who just doesn't listen, or a toddler who has constant tantrums. Whatever it is, usually, there is a fundamental reason it drives us insane as parents—we cannot control it. We like being in control, and now we're not. And the seething anger or crippling self-pity we've spent our lives hiding begins to be exposed.

This is important because what is being exposed is not your bad reaction to the situation—what is being exposed is *you*. The difficulty of parenting has torn us open, and we don't really like the heart we see inside ourselves.

There is an important theological truth here. Parenting shows us that we, like our children, are people whose greatest need is to be saved from ourselves.[1] Just like our children, our greatest danger is to be left to our own devices.

The Bible is remarkably blunt about how broken we are. Most of the patriarchs of the Bible were pretty rotten fathers. Other than Jesus, all of the biblical characters we meet are generally like us: people who botch most everything. None of them are particularly good, and when we idolize them, we do a disservice to one of the great themes of the Bible—that we are all failed sinners in desperate need of grace.

But this is only half of the main theme, and the second half is better. The good news is that Jesus loves us in the midst of our failures and is making broken people like us new again.

The tension between our failure and God's grace is foundational to the Bible, so it needs to be foundational to our parenting.

First, on our failure. Given who we know we are, it's silly to imagine that once we have kids, we'll get mature and stop being so sinful. Parenting, by itself, doesn't make us less selfish. On the contrary, the first thing it does is show us how selfish we really are.

And yet, in our failures, grace abounds! This is another way of saying that right at the moment we'd like to condemn ourselves, Jesus is doing the exact opposite—he is looking on us in gracious compassion and calling us to grow. This is grace in action, and it will never stop being counterintuitive to us. Grace means that

1. I am indebted to Paul David Tripp's excellent book *Parenting: Fourteen Gospel Principles That Can Radically Change Your Family* (Wheaton, IL: Crossway, 2016) for this key idea.

our failures don't have to set us back, they can call us forward. Grace means our mistakes aren't nearly so much opportunities to see how bad we are, but opportunities to see how good God is. Grace means that even though parenting by itself doesn't make us less selfish, parenting in the hands of God does—it sanctifies us.

This story of failure and grace in the Scriptures is so helpful to parenting. It means that every opportunity to parent through frustration and failure is not so much about what you're doing to your child as it is first about what God is doing in you. Every opportunity to parent is an opportunity to be parented by Jesus.

And generally, we are like Shep was that night: in need of someone to parent us into rest. Not rest in the crib but rest in our souls. Grace means that heart and soul, we can actually rest. The world is not on our shoulders (though parenting makes it feel like it always is) because Jesus on the cross bore the weight of the world for us.

That night, because of Jesus' grace, I got back up and went in and tried again. I held Shep like my heavenly father holds me, and in a matter of minutes, he was back at rest. That's what a good parent can do: settle the soul—and that's exactly what our heavenly father can do for us. Send us to bed with a settled soul.

I find that I need this reminder the most at the end of the day, when all of us are exhausted and running on reserves. This is when I need gospel liturgies to guide me into rest, body and soul.

But just like all these habits of the household, bedtime liturgies aren't solutions to make bedtime easy or prevent us from being bad parents, they are rhythms that remind us we can rest in God's goodness anyway. And we need those. Because otherwise we get stuck in our anger, our self-loathing, and our failures. That's why I try to repeat this statement as often as possible: Our habits won't change God's love for us, but God's love for us can and should change our habits.

If God's grace is really that good, it's worth building some habits at the end of the day to help us rest in that.

Bedtime Liturgies That Help Us Rest in the Work of Jesus

On a normal night, I still go to the Bedtime Blessing of Gospel Love I shared on page 6 to help us remind each other of God's grace in the evening. But many evenings are not nearly so serious, and ever since I began the habit of a blessing at bedtime, the list started to grow.

Some are ones for normal nights. Some are serious ones I use in special moments. Many are get-out-of-jail-free cards I use when things are getting crazy. But all of them guide us into some moment, however brief, of acknowledging God's love for us and inviting him to form our lives in that love and grace.

Tickle Blessing

First of all, far from being sanctimonious, these are usually fun. Nearly half the time when things go wrong or get silly, I simply revert to the tickle blessing. It has the advantage of getting them to the point of breathless laughter so you can get a sentence in.

....

A TICKLE BLESSING

Suddenly, and with lots of squirming:

Parent: Dear Lord, may this child find much joy and laughter, all of his/her days.
Child: *Uncontrollable laughter, until they can barely breathe*
Parent: Amen.

....

The tickle blessing is also useful for when you're in a serious mood, and they keep ruining it. For example, once in a while I'll say a prayer for them, and they keep interrupting, or deliberately saying words wrong, or throwing things at their brother. In those cases, the tickle blessing becomes a way to pivot—but without getting mad—and say, "Okay, two can play at this game." Then they get tickled until they can't take it.

Short Blessings Involving the Body

Similarly, when I think they just need a quick hug or a playful laugh, I'll squeeze them or bounce them. It works as a way to gain control of the situation and often turns misbehavior into laughter, which is better than discipline on most nights.

....

A BOUNCY BLESSING

While bouncing the bed around the child, and trying to get as much giggling and flopping as possible:

Parent: Dear Lord, may this child bounce from blessing to blessing, all of his/her days.
Child: *Bouncing and laughing*
Parent: Amen.

....

In general, these blessings remind me that the more physical you get, the more little kids can hang with you. Think of the way you can capture a one-year-old's attention by asking them where their nose is. Life is physical, and kids get that. I find the best way to greet my nieces is with a tight hug and a smile, and the best way to greet my nephews is with a laugh and a shove. In general there is something about the physical that pulls our minds in.

Consequently, I started a blessing that tracks their body. I like this one because while they get engaged with the body aspect of it, this has a more serious mood and often it leads to them asking questions about something I said.

It usually goes something like this:

A BLESSING FOR THE BODY OF A CHILD WHILE LYING IN BED

As prayer progresses, move hands to touch each part of the body:

Jesus, bless their feet, may they bring good news.
Bless their legs, may they carry on in times of suffering.
Bless their backs, may they be strong enough to bear the burdens of others.
Bless their arms to hold the lonely, **and their hands** to do good work.
Bless their necks, may they turn their heads toward the poor.
Bless their ears to discern truth, **their eyes** to see beauty, and **their mouths** to speak encouragement.
Bless their minds, may they grow wise.

And finally, bless their hearts, may they grow to love you—and all that you have made—in the right order.
Amen.

Liturgies as Ways to Let the Light Shine In

It is not unusual that we'll have friends over when the kids are going down. Once in a while they will come upstairs to say goodnight or maybe participate in the bedtime routine.

One time, my friend Matt was listening to our blessing for the body and said, "I wish Chris could be here. I feel like he might understand more of why we believe in God."

Chris (not his real name) is his close friend who is not a Christian.

This stuck with me because I felt like Matt was saying, "If only they could peer inside our houses and see that we actually believe this stuff, and that it's not for show, it's for love. If only they could see that it matters to our children, then maybe they'd be open to God."

I don't know if it's true, but I hope it is.

I want routines that poke holes in the ceiling of life so that the light of the divine can shine in. Whether it is our guests or our kids or ourselves, all of us need the reminder that the story we're living in is real, and it matters to our ordinary moments.

No one habit or blessing or prayer or conversation is going to magically change their life or relationship with God. That is (thank God!) up to the divine regeneration of the Holy Spirit (which allows us peace), but what these habits of the household are doing is giving our children windows into what we mean when we talk about faith.

We are giving them emotional anchors they can return to after they (as they surely will) wander off into the waters of their own heart. We are giving them words and rituals they can remember and turn over in their hands like a familiar heirloom when they inevitably encounter the confusing and contradictory words and rituals of the world.

I hope that someday someone will ask my children how to sum up the message of Jesus, and they will think back to bedtime and say, "Well, I suppose it's something like Jesus loves us, no matter what good or bad things we do." That would be a fine way of putting it, which is why I make it a point to recite it night after night.

I hope that one day when they suffer, instead of being surprised that life is hard, they think back to bedtime and pray, "Lord, make my legs strong to carry on in this time of suffering."

I hope that one day when their toddler is giving them the fits they gave me, they remember that they can tickle them and laugh instead of getting mad and shouting. And I do hope that they bounce from blessing to blessing all their days, which is why I pray it so often.

Prayer does, after all, change things. Especially us.

Leading Your Own Heart through Prayers for Your Kids

So back to little Shep. A year after the experience that brought me to my low, Shep was finally sleeping through the night, but he was still a wild beast.

Even now as I'm writing, he is a child who is all his own. He's got my olive skin, where the rest of our boys got my wife's fair skin. He's got dark hair, though the others are dirty blond. He's the smallest, but his mood dictates the mood of the room. He will not be left out—not ever.

Bedtime with him is usually so difficult and rowdy that while I felt I needed to be praying for Shep, it needed to be quick. Like, *really quick.*

So I started doing something very short. It went something like this:

A SHORT BLESSING FOR LITTLES

Perhaps with a sign of the cross on their head:

Parent: God loves you. Jesus died for you. And the Holy Spirit is with you. Goodnight.

Repetitive prayers with kids are always subject to physical improvisation. On nights when we're cheery, I punctuate each sentence with a big, ticklish kiss.

"Sheppard, God loves you." Attack with kiss. "And Jesus died for you." Attack with kiss. And so on. Other nights, I end with, "And Mama and Papa love you too."

But just when I'm tempted to think that these short, repetitive prayers don't matter, something happens and they blow my heart wide open. Like the other night with Shep.

Just a few weeks ago I was putting him to bed after a particularly terrible evening. That night, we had almost looked like a normal family—the kids helped clean the table and we all tried to play cards afterward—but Shep was darting around like a thief all night, removing the cups from the dishwasher we had just loaded, kicking swept piles, and (this is his new thing) popping the freezer drawer open, grabbing an ice cube, and sliding it across the floor.

It was one of those nights when you think, "This child is deliberately trying to invent new ways to infuriate me."

In the end, he started wrecking the cards the boys were playing with on the table, so I threw him over my shoulder and carried him up to bed an hour early—he was kicking and wiggling, yelling, "Turn! Turn!" (This is his toddler way of pleading for another chance.) I almost felt bad for him, but he was clearly cooked, and I was done too. As usual, I was mad.

I was struggling with actually believing that he was somehow trying to ruin our family, trying to mess everything up—that he himself was the problem, and if it just weren't for him . . . You get the point. I was looking at him in the opposite way that Jesus looks at him—and me.

When I put him in his crib, I didn't want to pray for him at all. But habits are powerful things, and I just started into my prayer, mostly involuntarily.

I began, "Sheppard, God loves you."

I paused at the startling words I just spoke, feeling a lump in my throat.

I say them every night. Every. Single. Night. Why the emotion now? What's different? I don't know, but I do know that prayers lead the heart. And suddenly the radical notion fell afresh. *God loves Sheppard.* Even now! More than I do. He adores him, even now in this age and stage. God is not distracted from Shep's "image of God-ness." God does not reduce Shep to Shep's defiant little toddler heart. He sees the fullness of all that he made and all that he will redeem. God is the father who loves him— and it hits me now—just the way he is.

So I looked at Shep and added, "God loves you just the way you are, so I promise to try to do the same."

Then I went on. "And Jesus died for you," and suddenly that part hit me too. Jesus is the sacrificial parent, giving up anything so his children can have everything—so I looked at Shep and added, "And I promise to sacrifice whatever it takes to love you too."

That was my version of repenting for the night.

And then I finished, "And just like the Holy Spirit is always with you, I will never leave you."

As can happen with a child snug in bed, suddenly the world softens, taking your heart with it, and Shep looked up at me, and knowing the end of the prayer, he mumbled through his pacifier, "Mama too." There he was, a wild little boy—but completely confident that God, Papa, and Mama all love him. Maybe we are doing something right.

"That's right," I said. "Mama loves you too, just like you are, and she'll never leave you either."

I walked back downstairs with the tears I needed in my eyes. My other sons were waiting at the table to restart the card game, but I was still swimming in the vows I just made to Shep—that no matter what the phase of the family, no matter what the stage of one of my children, I am here with them in covenant because God is with them in covenant. And if God loves them just the way they are, then so will I. And if Jesus gave up everything for them, then I can sacrifice too. And if the Holy Spirit is with us, then I'll never leave either.

I never thought of any of that when I started praying a short prayer for Shep. But God did. And the simple, rote prayer was there. Some words in the mouth to lead my own wild toddler of a heart, just when I needed it.

And that's what good habits do. God uses them to lead our hearts out of our own failures and into his grace, time and time again.

HABITS OF BEDTIME
FORMING CHILDREN

> **Main Idea**
>
> Bedtime is a moment, for parent and child, to acknowledge that at the end of the day, God loves us. No matter our failures, we can rest in grace. Bedtime liturgies use habitual prayers to find words (and actions) that incorporate the truths of the gospel into our routines—especially at the moments of the day when we are tired and the most likely to need them.

A Bedtime Blessing of Gospel Love

Said perhaps with a hand on your child's face or head.

Parent: Do you see my eyes?
Child: Yes.
Parent: Can you see that I see your eyes?
Child: Yes.
Parent: Do you know that I love you?
Child: Yes.
Parent: Do you know that I love you no matter what bad things you do?
Child: Yes.
Parent: Do you know that I love you no matter what good things you do?
Child: Yes.
Parent: Who else loves you like that?
Child: God does.
Parent: Even more than me?
Child: Yes.
Parent: Rest in that love.

A Tickle Blessing

Suddenly, and with lots of squirming:

Parent: Dear Lord, may this child find much joy and laughter, all of his/her days.
Child: *Uncontrollable laughter, until they can barely breathe*
Parent: Amen.

A BOUNCY BLESSING

While bouncing the bed around the child, and trying to get as much giggling and flopping as possible:

Parent: Dear Lord, may this child bounce from blessing to blessing, all of his/her days.
Child: *Bouncing and laughing*
Parent: Amen.

A SQUEEZE BLESSING

During a really big, really tight hug:

Parent: Dear Lord, may this child feel your love wrap around them, all of his/her days.
Child: *Struggles to break free and hopefully laughs*
Parent: Amen.

> **"In the story of God, coming to the end of ourselves isn't a sign of failure, it's the beginning of grace."**

A BLESSING FOR THE BODY OF A CHILD WHILE LYING IN BED

As prayer progresses, move hands to touch each part of the body:

Jesus, bless their feet, may they bring good news.
Bless their legs, may they carry on in times of suffering.
Bless their backs, may they be strong enough to bear the burdens of others.

Bless their arms to hold the lonely, **and their hands** to do good work.
Bless their necks, may they turn their heads toward the poor.
Bless their ears to discern truth, **their eyes** to see beauty, and **their mouths** to speak encouragement.
Bless their minds, may they grow wise.

And finally, bless their hearts, may they grow to love you—and all that you have made—in the right order.
Amen.

....

A Short Blessing for Littles When You Are Frustrated

Parent: God loves you. Jesus died for you. And the Holy Spirit is with you. Goodnight.

Pause for a deep breath, and a gentle touch.

Parent: So I too will love you. I too will sacrifice for you. And I too will never leave you.

....

A Nightly Parent's Prayer

Prayed just before the parent goes to bed, either beside the sleeping child's bed, or if they sleep lightly, then with an open palm held toward or against the sleeping child's door.

"Lord help me. May I be parented by your grace, and in turn give them the same. Amen."

A Note on Adapting

As kids get older, a tickle blessing might be more embarrassing than endearing. I still pray for my oldest before he goes to bed, though now I'm reaching up to put a hand on his head and looking him in the eye. Intentional words still matter.

We Always Need the Reminder of Grace: God's love inspires our action, but our action does not inspire God's love. Our family habits will not change God's love for us, but God's love for us should change our family habits.

PART 3

EPILOGUE

PARENTING BETWEEN THE

NOW AND THE NOT YET

I remember the day that I realized my children would grow old. I was on the way from a meeting and stopped at a coffee shop to wrap up a task. I had just sent the email to a client I needed to send, so my mind felt free for a moment.

"How old will Whit be when I am fifty?"

The question appeared in my head out of nowhere. If I were in a movie, some quiet rise of music would have snuck into the background. I was done with my work, so I entertained the question and I did the math in my head (which is no small feat for a lawyer like myself). I figured he would be about 23.

"What about Ash?"

"Okay," I thought, "I guess we're going to do them all." But no way was I doing more addition and subtraction in my head.

I often find moments of creativity come unexpectedly throughout the workday, so I always keep a notebook beside my laptop. Usually I just use it as a mousepad, but now I opened it up and began scribbling.

Here the soundtrack would have taken over. Because something was happening.

In the first column, I wrote down the ages for me and Lauren over the next twenty-five years. Then beside that, I wrote down Whit's corresponding ages. Then Asher's, Coulter's, and Shep's.

All at once, the music stopped. I put my pen down and stared at the page.

It was as if all of our lives were condensed to a single moment. I saw visions of my sons as teenagers and young men, new husbands and proud fathers. I saw them walking back in the door of our house, leaning down to hug Lauren. I saw a moment when I would be frail, and they would be strong—with them holding my hand, instead of vice versa.

I saw all of this at once and felt the weight of one of my favorite lines of T. S. Eliot's poetry that talks about "a lifetime burning in every moment."[1]

I had a moment of vision where the "now" intermingled with the "not yet."

Figure 3 is a picture of my journal that day.

As I'm sure you know, these moments are rare for parents in the thick of the childrearing years. You are tired, you are surrounded by diapers and laundry and deadlines, then sports practices, extracurriculars, and after-school pick-ups; you are worried about trying to make enough money, you are worried about paying for college, you are worried about the world they are going to encounter when they leave the house and the world technology is bringing into the house. The list goes on.

Sure, we may often think, "They are growing up so fast!" But if you are like me, then you equally as often think, "Parenting feels like it's taking forever!"

It can be hard to lift our tired minds out of the fog of the present. On most days, our vision of life is so shortsighted. It is of the next hour; at best, of the next day. But not much more.

---

1. T. S. Eliot, "East Coker," *Four Quartets* (London: Faber and Faber, 1940).

Figure 3

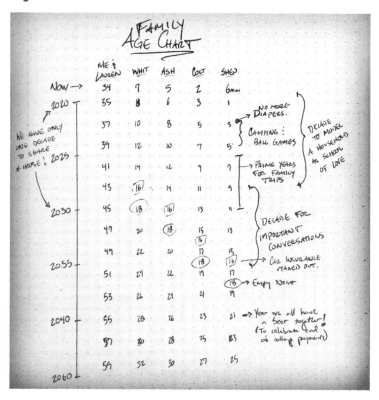

We keep our heads down because—after all—someone has to. That's what it takes to keep this all together.

And that's exactly why we need these kinds of vision moments so badly.

Proverbs says that "where there is no vision, the people perish."[2] Put another way, to keep our hearts alive, we need to see the future. We need to be in awe of the not yet. Because when we can see only the present, something inside of us starts to wither.

---

2. Prov. 29:18 KJV.

Staring at my age chart in the coffee shop with the imaginary soundtrack playing all around me, I had one of those rare moments when I could see a vision of the future. But it didn't make me feel scared, like time was running out.

I just felt the powerful sense that our time together was not forever. It was limited and more valuable because of that. I sensed the Lord saying to me, "Now is the time I have given for you to form them."

It reminded me that today I get the unique opportunity to help them become who they will be.

Parenting in Tension

In the story of God, we are meant to live in the tension of the now and the not yet. This is as hard as it is beautiful.

In the storyline of the world, we find ourselves in a curious moment. One great truth is that the world is fallen, but the other great promise is that God is making all things new in Jesus. And here we are, on a normal day, parenting our children under the cosmic tension of that painful and glorious truth. No wonder we feel something is amiss.

Let us begin honestly, then, with the pain. This is the now. And in the now, life is hard. Suffering is the norm. The truth is— as morbid as it may sound—we are all slowly dying. Parenting in the now means that all of our dreams don't amount to much. We had such high hopes for having kids, and now it seems more work than love. More exhaustion than fulfillment. Marriage is hard, work is hard, life is hard. Our bodies are changing, aging, and starting to break. Finding time with friends isn't easy anymore. At best, we feel tired. At worst, we feel trapped. In between, we feel lonely. And more likely than not, we feel bad about our parenting. We snap at our kids, we yell at them, we don't want to do this anymore. We're trying so hard, but they're disobeying, they're rebelling, they're drifting.

This isn't just you; this is me too. This is all of us. This is what it is like to parent in the now.

But one of the things you must know about the now is this: the very fact of your discontentment is a sign that you were meant for something else. Sit with that for a moment. We wish for a different world because we were made for a different world.[3]

This is a uniquely human struggle. A mama bear might be exhausted from scavenging food for her little ones, but after everyone has eaten, a mama bear doesn't experience existential angst about what it all means. She just goes to sleep with a full stomach.[4]

But not us humans. Not us fallen image-bearers. We know that life is more than surviving; we long for something else, even when we're not sure what it is. We long for a love we've never had but somehow sense is possible. We long for a *not yet*.

And this is the beautiful thing. The not yet is coming. This is the world made whole again. This is the world where you're no longer worried about your children's allergies or learning disabilities—because they're better now. Your parents are not dying anymore. They're here with you. In the not yet, you're not always at odds with your spouse. Your work has meaning, and you know it. Your body works, friendship is possible, and you are not alone. These are the kinds of things that will be true in the kingdom to come.

When we Christians say that God is making *all* things new,

---

3. C. S. Lewis, *Mere Christianity* (New York: Macmillan, 1952): "If I find in myself a desire which no experience in this world can satisfy, the most probable explanation is that I was made for another world."
4. See Bertrand Russell's Nobel lecture, "What Desires Are Politically Important?" on December 11, 1950, for more on this idea.

this is what we mean. That on the cross Jesus bore the final weight of the fall—so that we no longer have to. And when he rose again, he secured resurrection as the new reality. Now, he promises that when he comes again, he will do so to make all things new.[5] That is the world we're waiting for. That is the world we're destined for.

But as for today, living between the now and the not yet means that these two things are all mixed up. And while we must be firmly honest about the difficulties of the now, we must also be firmly committed to living in light of the not yet.

So it is the call of Christian parents to lift our eyes above the fog of the now and let the promise of the not yet inform our parenting today.

This means acknowledging that marriage is hard, but fighting for covenant love anyway. This means admitting that technology is a serious concern, but working to put meaningful limits on it. This means knowing that kids will always need to be disciplined, but committing to loving discipleship. This means coming to terms with the fact that life with children is a mess, but meals and play and family devotions are worth it anyway.

This means admitting that doing anything important is really hard and mostly marked by failure—for example, like practicing a rule of life for the habits of the household—but being convicted that it is worth trying anyway.

Trying to live into the not yet despite the now is an act of faith. And that's what Christians parent by: faith.

Good theology must always end in good practice. And if we are supposed to draw on visions of the not yet to inform our spiritual life now, then we should consider practices that help us do that on a regular basis.

---

5. Rev. 21:5.

Practicing Seeing the Now in Light of the Not Yet

I now keep the age chart in a journal that stays with me, because I want to be regularly reminded to work backward from a vision of the not yet to the habits of the now.

There are many ways to do this. For you, this might be taking the time to write out your family values or agree on a family motto. I know a lot of friends who have benefited much from making the time and space to think about the top five values of their family or creating a family motto that they all cling to. Perhaps this could be making a list of resolutions, five or so things your family is committed to doing over the long haul.

Whatever it is, these kinds of practices remind us of the glory of what we are called to do in parenting, but even more important, they also challenge us to act on that glory today. After all, now is the only moment we can act in. Have you ever thought about that?

You cannot change in the future. You can change only in the present because the present is the only moment you have access to. It is the only moment we can take action in.

You cannot start spending more time with your family next week; you can only do it this week, because whenever you get around to it, it will always be *this* week. Likewise, you can't tell your daughter you are sorry tomorrow; you can only do that today. You can't start making space to ask your wife important questions next month; you can only do it this month. You can't start making it on time to your kid's ball practice next time; you can only do it this time. Whenever we change, it will always be in the present tense.

So we must practice imagining the not yet in a way that calls us to change in the now. Writing out an age chart is one such practice. In the spirit of now being the moment for change, try it with me. I promise it will take only a few minutes of time, but it will give a few years of revelation.

1. Using the blank Family Age Chart in figure 4,[6] write down you and your spouse's ages in the first column.

2. In the space next to your column, write down the ages of each of your kids.

3. Now, in the space to the right of the chart, name some seasons you notice. When will you all be under the same roof? When will you be in the teenage season? When will be the best time to take trips? When will you need to be the most available for conversation?

4. Next, in light of what you see, at the bottom of the chart, write down two to three things you want to be true of your family. This is a space to dream. What kind of family is God calling you to be?

5. Finally, to the right of each dream, write down a corresponding habit. Remember, habits are small, concrete, repeating actions. But tiny habits can build enormous new realities. Maybe you want to use some of the habits in this book, or maybe you have your own ideas. Either way, write down some of the kinds of things you would do each day or week to live into this vision of the future.

6. Now, pray. Ideally, do this with your spouse or show this to your spouse and pray together about it. Maybe use it for a parenting check-in on a date night. Whatever you do, don't leave this page sitting alone in this book. Tear it out or take a picture. Print a copy and keep it on your desk or your refrigerator.

---

6. Or if you prefer, you can find this template online at https://www.habitsofthehousehold.com/familyagechart.

FIGURE 4. FAMILY AGE CHART

Year	Your Age	Children's Ages	Seasons
	. . . .	. . . .	
	. . . .	. . . .	
	. . . .	. . . .	
	. . . .	. . . .	
	. . . .	. . . .	
	. . . .	. . . .	
	. . . .	. . . .	
	. . . .	. . . .	
	. . . .	. . . .	
	. . . .	. . . .	
	. . . .	. . . .	
	. . . .	. . . .	
	. . . .	. . . .	
	. . . .	. . . .	
	. . . .	. . . .	
	. . . .	. . . .	
	. . . .	. . . .	

Future Realities   **Habits for Today**

→

→

→

Someone Who Loved Us into Loving

Understanding that we parent in the tension between the now and the not yet reminds us that formation is a long game. It does not happen overnight. The now means that our efforts in the present are far more marked by failure than by success. But in light of the not yet, we can rest assured that that is okay, and the fight for formation is worth it.

It reminds us that as important as habits of the household are, our motivation is not what we can accomplish through them in the now. Our motivation is what God will accomplish in the not yet.

I see this in my own story.

When I was young, I remember waking up most days and coming upstairs to find my dad reading his Bible in his study. When I imagine a morning in my house, I imagine him there, with his desk lamp on and his big leather Bible spread open in front of him where he noted things in the margin.

Twenty-some years later, that Bible now lives on my desk. He gave it to me sometime during college. A couple of years ago, as I was writing my first book, *The Common Rule*,[7] I was writing about the habit of reading Scripture, and I remembered my dad in his study.

Out of curiosity, I opened his big leather Bible and came to Colossians, where there was a series of dates written down across the page. "January 7, 2002" was written next to chapter 1, "January 8, 2002" was written next to chapter 2, and so on.

The first thing that struck me was that these mornings he spent in Colossians were in the days following his loss of the

---

7. I tell a version of this story in chapter 4 of *The Common Rule: Habits of Purpose for an Age of Distraction.*

governor's race in Virginia. I'll never forget how hopeful I was that he would win and how crushed I was when he didn't. But I'll also never forget how steady he was through the whole thing. The morning after his November loss, I remember him having pancakes ready for us when we woke and telling us about what he had read in the Bible that morning.

Only years later would I realize that most likely the reason my dad was able to keep such a steady identity through those political seasons of ups and downs was because his career didn't define him, the love of his heavenly father did. I don't think he needed to look to the world for love because he knew who he was in God's love. I'm sure catching a glimpse of that father's love every morning in the Scriptures helped with that, which is one reason I cannot stop writing about it.

But the second thing that I noticed was even more significant. Written next to all of those dates in Colossians was something else—it was my name.

I was a senior in high school at the time, and I was already living those years I told you about earlier—with a lot of mistakes and a lot of secrets. I was in the thick of my own rebellion. It was a time when I genuinely believed I could guide my life better than my dad or Jesus or anyone else could.

I'm sure this caused no small amount of pain for my mom and dad. After they put in all those years of work and formation, I was throwing it all away. I often think about how the gospel posture of a parent is opening yourself up to be hurt by your children, while committing to loving them anyway. That's what Jesus did for us, after all.

To say the least, at that time, I wasn't very open to my dad's parenting. And yet I remember it was during that time that my dad would gently invite me, over and over, to get up early with him and read the Bible.

Sometimes I would say no and sleep in. Sometimes I would say yes. Sometimes I would doze off during our readings and prayers.

To be honest, I don't remember a single verse we read. I don't remember a single prayer we prayed. But I will tell you what I do remember. What I do remember was the sense that I had a dad who loved me when I was the most unlovable. What I remember was sitting next to him reading about a God who loves us—a God whose love makes us lovable.

It would be two years later that I finally had the conversation with him in Toronto that began to change my life. During that season, when I finally became convicted that I didn't like who I was becoming, I couldn't help but think about who my dad was. I thought of him as someone who was becoming more like Jesus. And in the end, after trying out my own path and failing miserably, that was who I wanted to be too.

"Follow me as I follow Christ," Paul wrote.[8] In the end, I followed Jesus by following my dad.

There is a beautiful tension here. In the final analysis, it is neither us nor our habits that form our children, it's Jesus' grace. He is the one who walks with them through their best and their worst days. Just like he has done for us. That's a big relief for us parents.

And yet, Jesus uses us. And he uses our habits too. He uses who we are to form who our children will be. And that's not a burden, that's a blessing, because it means our actions matter. We don't have to bear the weight of being finally responsible for who our children are. But we can carry the joy that what we do has meaning. It is not lost, and God will make use of it.

The final role of a parent is just to be someone who keeps

---

8. 1 Cor. 11:1 MEV.

looking to Jesus. As you do that, your children will be looking at you. Then you just point up and smile, saying, "See, there's the father who loves us. Let's both become like him."

I started this book with a claim that we become our habits and our kids become us, so we should care about habits of the household. I hope you now see that the whole idea is predicated on our looking to Jesus. By doing that, we become like Jesus, and our kids become like us, and in this connection of holy imitations, we all follow him together.

In the last years of Fred Rogers' life, he gave a graduation speech where he reminded us that we all learn the most important things by imitation: "From the time you were very little, you've had people who have smiled you into smiling, people who have talked you into talking, sung you into singing, loved you into loving."

And it's true, of course. For all of us, someone has. His name is Jesus. And the idea of cultivating habits of the household is nothing more than cultivating rhythms of looking at the God who is always looking back at us.

He is the one who smiles us into smiling and loves us all into loving.

ACKNOWLEDGMENTS

While musing about the importance of extended families, Kurt Vonnegut once wrote, "You are not enough people." It's true. I am not.

While musing about being in love, Ben Folds once wrote, "I am the luckiest." It's true. I am.

I am not enough people, but I'm still the luckiest, because I have Lauren. Raising a family with her has been the most fun, the most hard, and the most sanctifying thing I have ever done and probably will ever do. I wouldn't have a single experience worth sharing if it wasn't for her. What's more, if it wasn't for her (ruthless!) editing, it might be worth sharing, but not worth reading. I am the author, but she is forever the muse.

As much as I love Lauren, we are still not enough people. But luckily, we have you, Mom and Dad. And you too, Fred and Teresa. I began this book with a quip often attributed to Frederick Douglass, that it is easier to raise strong children than to repair broken men and women. What an inheritance you all have given Lauren and me, and our boys, by being parents who accepted God's covenant love, loved each other with an echo of that covenant love, and put both on display for us. And what an inheritance my sons get to grow up with such holy, wise, loving, and fun grandparents.

A wife and parents are one thing, but it's still not enough

people! So to Rachel and David, Mark and Mary Alice, Dan and Mary Catherine, Frank and Christine, and Anne—I am lucky to call my family friends. What a gift we have in all these children of ours. Let's continue to raise good disciples of Jesus who are also good friends to each other too. See you all at lunch this Sunday.

And finally, to my friends in Richmond (and DC, and Shanghai, etc.), whom I am lucky enough not to have space here to name. It is such a glory to be able to raise children together. To all your examples, mostly unspoken, I am so indebted. I am lucky to call my friends family.

After all, I am not enough people.